Acoustic Guitar for Adults

with Video Play-Along Method for Easy Strumming Success

Andy Schneider

See streaming video access instructions on the last page of this book

Play Along with this Book!

Stream the free video examples of these exercises

Scan and go now

SEEINGMUSICBOOKS.COM

SEEING MUSIC
METHOD BOOKS

Welcome from Your Instructor

Hello my new friend,

I love learning. It's my lifelong passion.

I'm glad to see you here, an adult learner just like me. Maybe you've tried learning before. Maybe today is your first day thinking about playing guitar. Welcome.

If you've picked up this book, chances are you have a burning passion to learn the guitar, perhaps a passion that has been simmering for years or even decades. You might be wondering, "Am I too late to start?" or "Is it possible for someone like me, with no prior musical knowledge, to play the guitar?" I'm here to tell you: it's never too late, and yes, you absolutely can.

Over the years, I've had the pleasure of guiding countless adults, just like you, through their first chords, songs, and performances. Many came to me with doubts, believing they lacked the "musical gene" or were too old to pick up an instrument. But time and time again, I've seen the magic that unfolds when dedication meets guidance. Each of them, with commitment and patience, unlocked the world of music that lay waiting in their hearts.

This book has been meticulously crafted to cater to adult beginners. It's not just a collection of lessons, but a compass—guiding you from the foundational postures and notes, through the nuances of chords and melodies, and into the realm of making music that resonates with your soul. Each chapter is a stepping stone, building upon the previous, ensuring a smooth transition from one skill to the next.

Remember, every accomplished guitarist started somewhere, often with the same doubts and questions you might have now. But what they all had in common was a spark—a desire to create, to express, and to bring joy through music. With this book as your guide and your own passion as the driving force, you too can embark on a fulfilling musical journey.

Whether your dream is to strum along to your favorite songs, write your own melodies, or simply enjoy the therapeutic effects of playing an instrument, you're in the right place. I've been fortunate to help many adults find their rhythm, and now, it's your turn. Let's tune up, dive in, and uncover the guitarist within you.

Your best music is still inside of you, so let's get started!

Andy Schneider

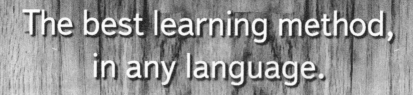

The best learning method, in any language.

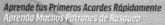

Contents

Foundations of Guitar Playing: Posture, Tuning and Strumming

GREAT GUITAR PLAYING BEGINS WITH GREAT POSTURE AND INSTRUMENT POSITIONING. YOU'LL FIND IT MUCH EASIER TO REACH THOSE CHORD FINGERINGS.

READ THIS FIRST: START WITH GREAT POSTURE

It may seem trivial, but great guitar playing requires good posture. After you align your body and arms, you'll find playing much easier.

FIG.1 - PROPER GUITAR POSITION

Grab the right chair: You'll need to select a chair that keeps your thighs parallel to the ground. Hold your guitar close, allowing the neck to angle slightly upward. This positioning aids in keeping your left hand roughly aligned with your right elbow. If the neck droops, the left hand's reach increases, making playing both challenging and awkward. It's tempting to just flop on the couch with your instrument, but it's really hard to play well that way!

Start with your feet: Elevate your right heel a tiny bit, raising the guitar by about an inch. Observe the position of your left thumb—it should be directly behind the guitar's neck. Coupled with a straight wrist, this alignment is a great start towards good guitar technique. Though maintaining a straight wrist might pose initial challenges, its importance will unveil itself in the subsequent lessons.

Tune and Re-tune: Continually revisit this chapter and reorient your posture as needed. Perfecting basics now speeds up your journey to expertise later.

FIG.2 - GOOD HAND POSITION

TIME FOR A TUNE-UP: ALL ABOUT TUNING

Tuning is the first step to ensuring your guitar sounds as it should, offering rich and harmonious tones. Playing on an out-of-tune guitar is no fun. Here's a little background about the often overlooked subject of tuning.

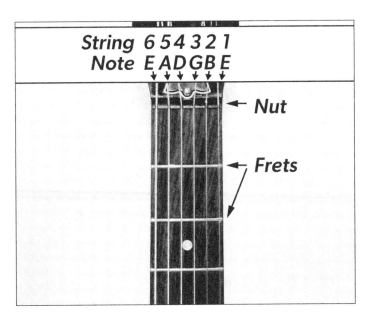

FIG.3 - STANDARD GUITAR TUNING

Common Guitar Tunings

Standard	E A D G B E
Std. Lowered	E♭ A♭ D♭ G♭ B♭ E♭
DADGAD	D A D G A D
Drop D	D A D G B E
Open G	D G D G B D

FIG.4 - COMMON GUITAR TUNING STYLES

Standard Tuning

You may have heard that some guitarists tune their guitars a little differently than usual. Indeed, there are many different ways to tune the same instrument to acheive different results. Let's look at some of them.

Standard Guitar Tuning: This book uses **Standard Tuning**, which starting from the thickest string (far from the ground) to the thinnest string (closest to the ground), is: E, A, D, G, B, and E.

Non-Standard Tuning

Yes, if there is a Standard Tuning, there must be a non-Standard, too! In fact, there are many, many different ways to tune the guitar. While 99% of guitar music is performed in Standard Tuning, non-standard varieties offer a different sound and opportunities for some creative chords. It should be noted that when playing in non-standard tunings, all of the chords require different fingerings. For this reason, it's best to learn guitar using Standard Tuning, and leave the advanced stuff for a bit later.

Dear DAD: One of the most common non-standard tunings is **DADGAD**, which as you might guess, tunes the guitar D, A, D, G, A, D. This tuning is favorited by blues guitarists and those wishing to play with a slide.

Drop it! Another interesting tuning is **Drop-D**, which is (lowest to highest) D, A, D, G, B and E. Notice how it's identical to Standard tuning, except for the lowest string lowered from E, down one whole-step to D. It's a big rock favorite.

Eb Standard: This is a fun one, favorited by Classic Rock bands like Guns and Roses and Jimi Hendrix. It's a modified version of Standard Tuning where every string is lowered

1/2 step. It goes, E-flat, A-flat, D-flat, G-flat, B-flat, E-flat. Since all the strings are less tight than in Standard, it has a more relaxed feel and a bit darker tone.

Electronic Tuners

Device Type: These are standalone devices, usually pocket-sized, designed exclusively for tuning acoustic or electric stringed instruments.

How to Use: Simply turn it on and, if a clip-on type, clip it to your guitar's headstock. If the unit offers a standard guitar jack and your guitar has a pickup, plug them together so the pickup is sent to the tuner. Pluck a string, and the tuner will display the note you're closest to and whether you're flat (too low), sharp (too high), or in tune.

Advantage: They often come with built-in microphones and the clip-on type can be used in noisy environments, thanks to the clothespin-type attachment feature which detects vibrations directly from the guitar.

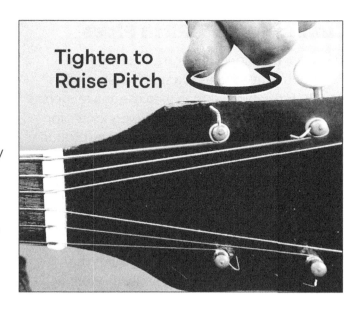

Fig.5 - Raising Pitch (on Most Guitars)

Tuning Apps for Devices

Device Compatibility: Many modern tuning apps are available for smartphones and tablets.

How to Use: After downloading and opening the app, you'll typically pluck a string, and the app will use your device's microphone to listen and guide you to the correct pitch. Have a look through your phone or device's app store. The free versions are often sufficient for standard tuning, while the premium versions may offer alternate tunings, chord libraries, and more.

Advantage: The convenience of always having a tuner on your phone. Many apps also come with additional features like metronomes or chord libraries.

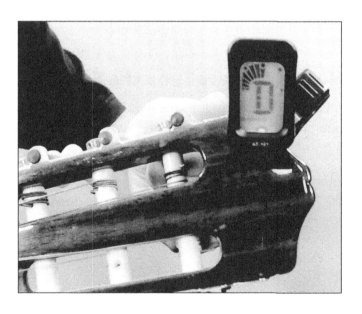

Fig.6 - Using a Clip-On Electronic Tuner

Tuning by Ear

For seasoned players or those training their ears, you can tune the guitar to itself or another instrument like a piano. Start with one string in tune (often the A or E string), and adjust the other strings relative to that. While this method can be tricky for beginners, it's a valuable skill for any musician.

Tuning Forks & Pitch Pipes

These are traditional methods. A tuning fork, when struck, resonates at a specific pitch (often A=440 Hz), which you can then use as a reference. Pitch pipes are little, harmonica-like gadgets for tuning reference. When blown into, they produce the note you need to match.

Tips for Successful Tuning

Always Tune UP to a Note: If you go past the desired pitch, lower the string's pitch and then tune up to the correct note. This ensures the string's tension is even and stays in tune longer.

Stretching It: - New strings stretch and may go out of tune more frequently at first. Regular tuning and playing can help them stabilize faster.

Whether you're tuning by ear, using a device, or an app, regularly checking and adjusting your guitar's tuning is crucial. Over time, you'll become faster and more accurate, ensuring your guitar always sounds its best.

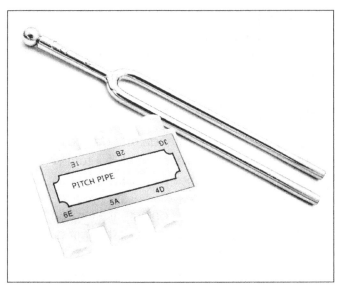

Fig.7 - Pitch Pipe and Tuning Fork

Tuning by Ear?

As your perception of pitch develops, your ears will become great detectors of pitch. This takes a little while, but is a skill worth developing.

Not All Guitars Tune the Same Way

A Word of Caution: Not all guitars have tuning machines that tighten in the same direction. There have been a few that work backwards. On those guitars, turning the keys counter-clockwise doesn't loosen the string, but actually tightens it.

Either way, it's a good idea to always pick the string and listen as you start to turn the key. Make sure the pitch is going the correct direction, up or down.

ABOUT GUITAR STRINGS

The guitar strings are labeled based on their pitch and thickness: the thinnest, highest-pitched string is the first, while the thickest, lowest-pitched one is the sixth.

The Evolution of Guitar Strings

Ancient guitar strings were made from the intestines of sheep, known as *catgut*. Despite the name, no kitties were harmed:)

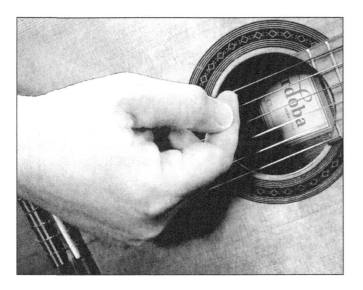

FIG.8 - STRUMMING WITH A FINGER

Guitar body size and shape both help scupt the instrument's tone.

STRUMMING: PICKS VS. FINGERS

Depending on your guitar type, strumming varies. Using a pick provides precision and allows for varied techniques. Hold the pick between your thumb and index finger, ensuring a small portion protrudes. Strumming downwards or upwards produces distinct sounds; practice both.

For classical guitars, which are characterized by their nylon strings, finger-strumming is more traditional. Your thumb, index, middle, and ring fingers each play a role. Alternatively, classical guitarists sometimes use very light picks for certain tones. The goal is to maintain fluidity and precision. As you advance, your fingers or the pick become an extension of your musical expression, allowing you to create melodies that resonate.

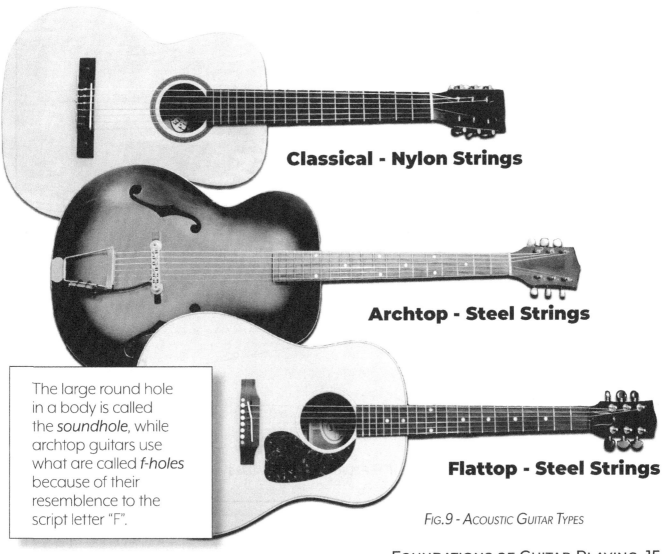

Classical - Nylon Strings

Archtop - Steel Strings

The large round hole in a body is called the *soundhole*, while archtop guitars use what are called *f-holes* because of their resemblence to the script letter "F".

Flattop - Steel Strings

FIG.9 - ACOUSTIC GUITAR TYPES

ACOUSTIC GUITAR DIAGRAM

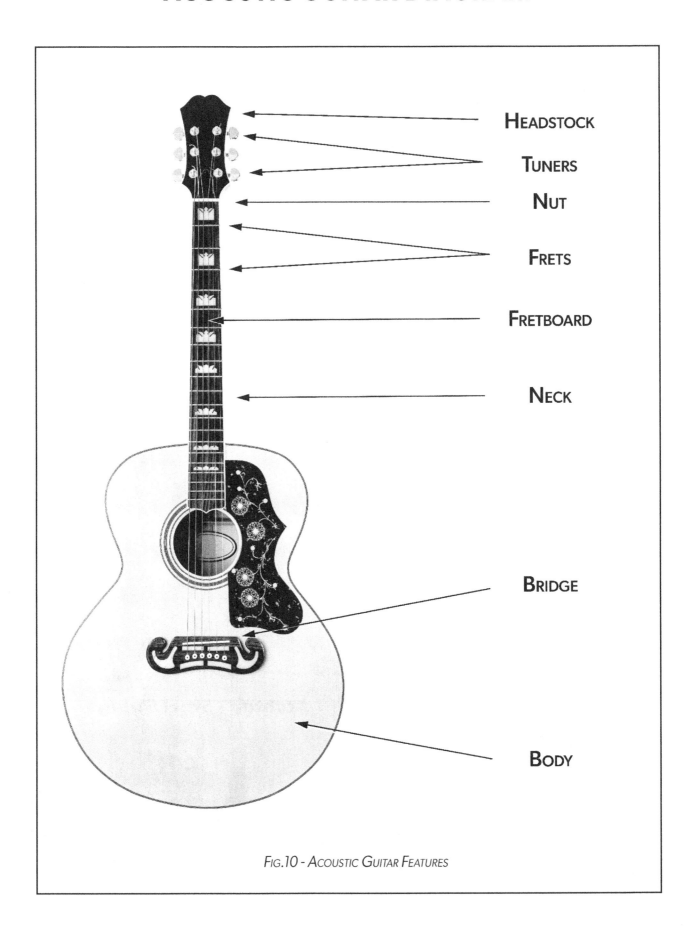

HEADSTOCK

TUNERS

NUT

FRETS

FRETBOARD

NECK

BRIDGE

BODY

FIG.10 - ACOUSTIC GUITAR FEATURES

How to Read Chord Diagrams: A Beginner's Guide

CHORD DIAGRAMS ARE VISUAL REPRESENTATIONS THAT INDICATE HOW TO PLAY CHORDS ON THE GUITAR. THEY SERVE AS A ROADMAP FOR FINGER PLACEMENT ON THE FRETBOARD.

CHORD DIAGRAM BASICS

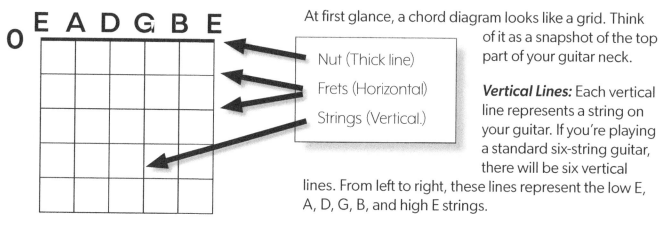

Fig.11 - Open-String Names

At first glance, a chord diagram looks like a grid. Think of it as a snapshot of the top part of your guitar neck.

Vertical Lines: Each vertical line represents a string on your guitar. If you're playing a standard six-string guitar, there will be six vertical lines. From left to right, these lines represent the low E, A, D, G, B, and high E strings.

Horizontal Lines: These lines represent the frets on the guitar neck. The topmost line often indicates the nut of the guitar. In this book, a "0" is written beside the nut.

Black Dots: These dots tell you where to place your fingers. The placement of the dot corresponds to the location, string, and fret of your finger.

Numbers Inside Dots: Some chord diagrams will have numbers inside the dots. These numbers indicate which finger to use. (1 = index finger, 2 = middle finger, 3 = ring finger, 4 = pinky finger)

X's and O's: Above the diagram, you might see the shapes of "X" or "O" aligned with certain strings. An "X" means that you won't play that string. An "O" means you should play the string open, without adding any fret fingers.

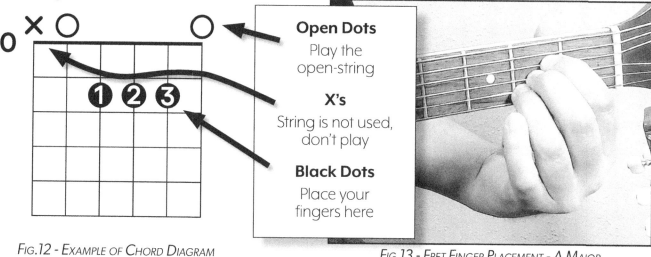

Fig.12 - Example of Chord Diagram

Fig.13 - Fret Finger Placement - A Major

HOW TO READ CHORD DIAGRAMS

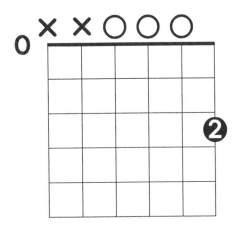

FIG.14 - DIAGRAM - G MAJOR EASY

1 Start by examining the chord diagram, beginning with the bottom of the chord, the lowest pitched string. It's the 6th string E, which appears as the vertical line on the left. It corresponds to your lowest-pitched guitar string, the one furthest from the floor. Is there a note to be played on the 6th string? How about the 5th? In the sample chord here, G Major Easy, there are no black dots on those strings, only X's above them. What's an X mean? See Step 2!

2 Check for any X's or O's. X's indicate strings that aren't used, while O's mark open-strings. In this chord, strings 6 and 5 are not played, indicated by the X's over those strings. Strings 4, 3 and 2 are played open as indicated by the O's.

3 If the string has a black dot, place your corresponding finger on that string near that fret. Placing your finger near the fret produces the best sound. In this chord, the 2nd finger presses at the 3rd fret. This is the 1st string, high E. It is the string closest to the ground.

FIG.15 - G MAJOR EASY - HAND POSITION

4 Strum the chord to hear how it sounds.If you'd like to try this chord, don't forget to avoid strumming the 6th and 5th strings (marked by X's).

PRACTICAL TIPS FOR READING CHORD DIAGRAMS

Orientation: Always ensure that you're viewing the chord diagram with the correct orientation. The vertical lines represent your guitar strings, with the line nearest the starting-fret number, corresponding to your low E string.

Barre Chords: In this book, barred fretting (when a finger is layed across the strings, playing multiple notes at once) are indicated by several dots, all with the same finger number inside them. Outside of this book, you might encounter a chord diagram displayed as a curved line across multiple strings. This indicates a barre chord, where one finger (usually the index) presses down on multiple strings simultaneously.

Chord Name: When sheet music contains chord charts, the name of the chord is typically written above the chord diagram. Not all sheet music has chord charts for guitar. Some charts have just the chord name. Familiarize yourself with common chord names like G Maj (G Major), Dmin (D minor), A7, C Maj7 (C Major 7). These are all found later in this book.

As you gain experience, you'll have these chords committed to memory and won't always need chord chart sheet music.

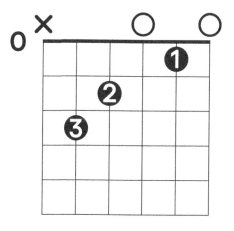

FIG.16 - C MAJOR - FULL

FIG.17 - C MAJOR - FULL HAND POSITION

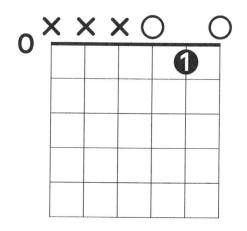

FIG.18 - C MAJOR - EASY

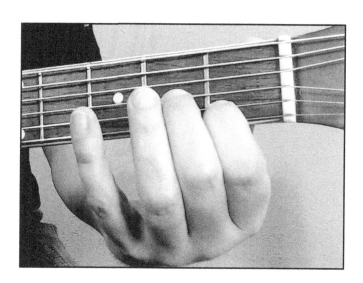

FIG.19 - C MAJOR - EASY HAND POSITION

LEARNING BONUS - MEMORIZE YOUR STRINGS

Elephants
And
Donkeys
Grow
Big
Ears

Be sure you memorize the names of your strings. Here's a quick way to easily remember them.

The strings of the guitar are, in order (Lowest to Highest): E, A, D, G, B and E

Just remember:
Elephants and Donkeys Grow Big Ears!

ABOUT CHORD NAMES AND SYMBOLS

CHORD NAMES AND SYMBOLS ARE WRITTEN IN SEVERAL FORMS, WHICH CAN SOMETIMES MAKE LEARNING THEM PRETTY CONFUSING. HERE'S A WAY TO BREAK DOWN THOSE CHORD SYMBOLS AND GET THEIR MEANING, EVERY TIME.

Every chord has a root note and every chord has a flavor, such as Major or Minor. To keep the names simple, the flavor will often be omitted if the chord is Major. Instead of "C Major", you could just say "C".

Here you can see the most common ways to indicate a C Major chord and an A minor chord.

Notice that if real simplicity is needed, only one letter might be used. If major, the single letter abbreviation is capitalized. If the chord is minor, the single letter symbol is not capitalized. As with "C" and "a", shown in the figure.

$$C \quad Cmaj \quad C^{\triangle}$$

$$a \quad Am \quad Amin \quad A^{-}$$

FIG. 20 - CHORD NAME EQUIVALENTS

To add more sonic color and variety, some chords use extensions. These additional notes build on the basic minor or major chord. The extension is awritten at the end of the chord symbol.

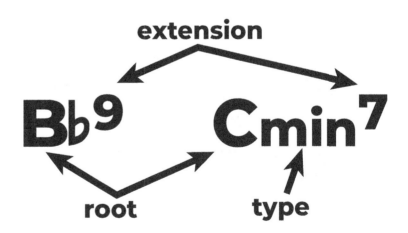

You'll be learning some extended chords later in this book. If you're curious about extensions and how to use them, check out *Guitar Theory Nuts and Bolts* from Seeing Music.

Start at Square One: Play Single Notes Cleanly

GOOD ACOUSTIC WORK MEANS PLAYING CLEANLY AND WITH ACCURACY. BEFORE DIVING INTO WHOLE CHORDS, TAKE A MINUTE TO CHECK OUT YOUR NOTES INDIVIDUALLY.

PLAY JUST ONE NOTE

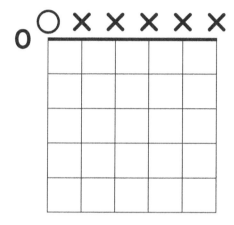

FIG. 21 - OPEN E

Remember the notes from the earlier lesson that acquainted you with the string names? Begin with your lowest-string, open E. With your right-hand thumb or a pick, play the open E on the 6th string. This is the biggest sounding note on your guitar and it's charged with lots of sonic energy.

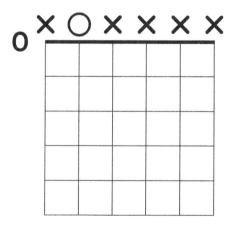

FIG. 22 - OPEN A

Next, focus on the open A. It's beneficial to glance at your picking hand to ensure you're precisely striking the 5th string. It's common to accidentally hit adjacent strings, so maintain precision to target just the A string.

FRETTING WITH PRECISION

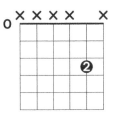

FIG.23 - 1ST STRING - G

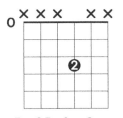

FIG.24 - 2ND STRING - D

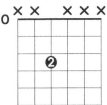

FIG.25 - 3RD STRING - B FLAT

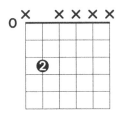

FIG.26 - 4TH STRING - F

FIG.27 - 5TH STRING - C

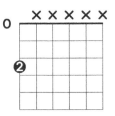

FIG.28 - 6TH STRING - G

HOLD YOUR GUITAR IN GOOD PLAYING POSITION. IF NECESSARY, REVISIT THE CHAPTER "FOUNDATIONS OF GUITAR PLAYING".

1 Starting with the 1st String (the one closest to the ground) find the 3rd fret. The nut is considered "0", the first fret is 1, then count 2, then 3. Place your finger between the 2nd and 3rd frets, very close to the 3rd. You should be right up against the fret, but not on top of it for the best sound. Play this note. It is the 1st String note, G.

2 You can release that note. Now similarly, The 2nd string's 3rd fret is the note D. Use your fretting hand's 2nd finger here, too.

3 Now, move your fretting finger over one string to the 3rd string. At the 3rd fret, play B-flat.

4 Again, moving over one string, play the 4th string F.

5 Now again move to the next string, 5th string C.

6 Finally, play the 6th string G.

Now, reset your finger to the 1st string and repeat these steps several times. Go slowly and accurately.

How does that sound? It's a very simple exercise, but an important one.

PERFECT YOUR TONE

How's the resonance? Any unwanted buzzing? A rich, clear note is the aim. Most learners require consistent practice before achieving clean notes. If there are issues, ensure your finger is proximate to the fret – almost atop it. This positioning is vital and once mastered, simplifies subsequent learning.

Ensure your wrist remains straight. Elevating the neck and keeping the fretboard close to your shoulder assists in this. Always ensure comfort; if there's discomfort or pain, pause immediately. It's natural for beginners to experience fingertip soreness, but over time, calluses form, alleviating this.

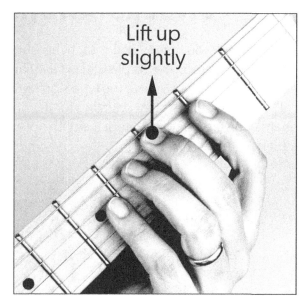

Fig.29 - Left-Hand Muting

STRING DYNAMICS

Notes have start and endpoints. While initiating a note remains consistent, there are two techniques to halt it. For instance, begin with open A followed by open E. Start each using a pick or thumb and halt by lightly touching the string with your fretting fingers. The same applies to fretted notes like C and G – release your fretting finger pressure to silence them.

Alternatively, mute using your picking hand, known as palm muting. It's akin to braking in a vehicle. After striking a note, use the fleshy portion between your pinky and wrist to mute it. Experiment with varying speeds and see the results.

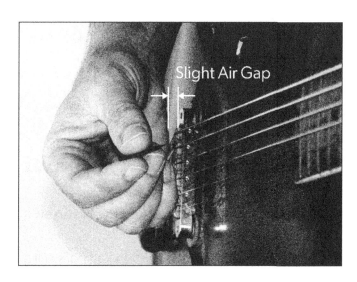

Fig.30 - Picking Position

Notice the very, very subtle touch the side of the palm gives the strings when needing to stop their ringing.

In the middle photo at right, there is a slight separation between the palm and strings.

In the lower photo, the palm has lightly contacted the strings, muting them.

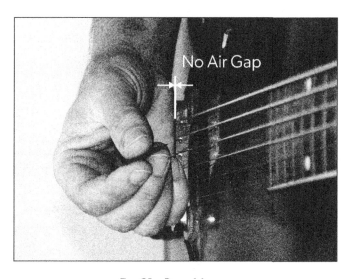

Fig.31 - Palm Muting

UNDERSTANDING STAFF NOTATION

Musical staffs tell you how to count each measure (or *bar*) of the music. Here, a Treble Clef with a time signature is illustrated. The Treble Clef (a fancy or curly "G" shape) indicates the range of notes (Bass Clef notes are lower pitched), while the time signature guides counting. In 4/4 time, the musician counts "1, 2, 3, 4" and then repeats that counting for the next measure. The bottom number 4, signifies that quarter notes are what are being counted. If eighth notes are being counted, the number would be 8. If half notes, it is 2.

Fig.32 - 4/4 Time Signature

Think of each measure as a container that holds a <u>specific</u> number of musical notes or beats of a <u>specific</u> type. In the case of 4/4 time, there are 4 beats per measure (that's the top number) and each beat is a quarter note (that's the bottom number).

FAQ: Understanding Note Types and Rhythms

Whole note: Lasts for 4 beats. Just one fills an entire measure in 4/4 time.

Half note: Lasts for 2 beats. So, two half notes fill a measure in 4/4.

Quarter note: Lasts for 1 beat. You can fit four of these in one measure of 4/4.

Eighth notes: These are half the length of a quarter note, so they last for half a beat. It takes eight of these to fill a measure.

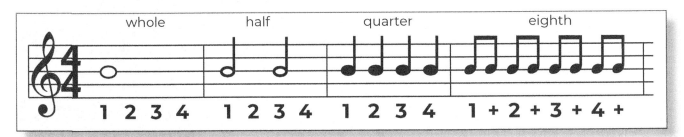

Fig.33 - Note Types

Rests: Just like there are notes of different lengths, there are also rests of different lengths. Rests are moments of silence where no note is played, but they still take up space in our "container". So, if you see a rest, it means you don't play a note for that beat or beats, but you will count them in your rhythm.

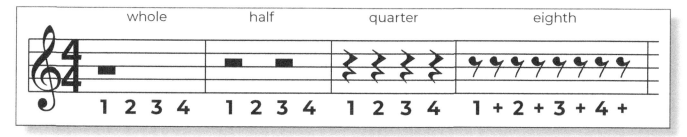

Fig.34 - Various Rest Types

Notice how the half and whole rests look a lot alike? The whole rest hangs below the staff line; the half sits above it. Some students remember them this way: Whole notes resemble a hole in the ground, while the half-note looks a bit like a hat. "Half" sounds like "hat". Just remember "Whole rests are like holes, Halves are like Hats."

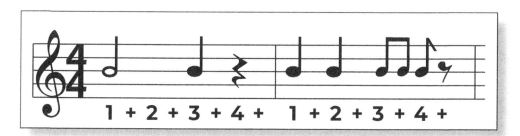

Fig.35 - Mixed Value Notes and Rests

And most importantly, a measure can be filled with a mix of any of these note or rest types, as long as they total the number of beats indicated in the time signature.

Study the 2nd measure, beats 3 and 4. There are three eighth notes and one eighth rest. Sometimes eighth notes are tied together at the top, as in beat 3. Because only one eighth note is used in the fourth beat, the flag at the top of the eighth note is angled down.

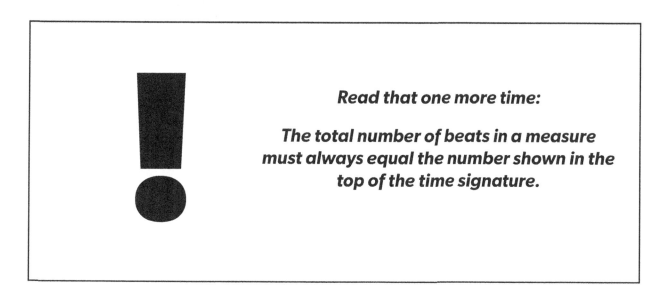

Read that one more time:

The total number of beats in a measure must always equal the number shown in the top of the time signature.

Reading and Playing Measures

When reading music with a 4/4 time signature:

1 Start at the beginning of the measure.

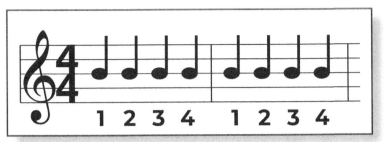

Fig.36 - Two Measures of Quarter Notes

2 Count each beat as you play. You can softly count, "1, 2, 3, 4" to ensure you're giving each note or rest its proper length.

3 When you reach the end of one measure (after the 4th beat), move on to the next one and continue counting.

Subdividing Beats

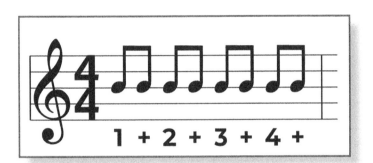

Fig.37 - One Measure of Eighth Notes

Sometimes it's helpful to count rhythms with more precision than just "1, 2, 3, 4". For example, this measure of eighth notes is counted "1 and, 2 and, 3 and, 4 and". The "plus" sign is used when writing down "and".

By understanding the 4/4 time signature and how beats are divided in a measure, you'll have a solid foundation to start reading and playing music. Just remember to keep counting and make sure everything adds up to 4 in each measure!

Fretting with Ease

Don't press too hard when fretting. It can cause notes to be "bent" out-of-tune and also causes unnecessary hand strain.

SINGLE-NOTE EXERCISES

Practice producing and then silencing notes. The staff's beats denote the moment to play the chord, which is stated above that measure.

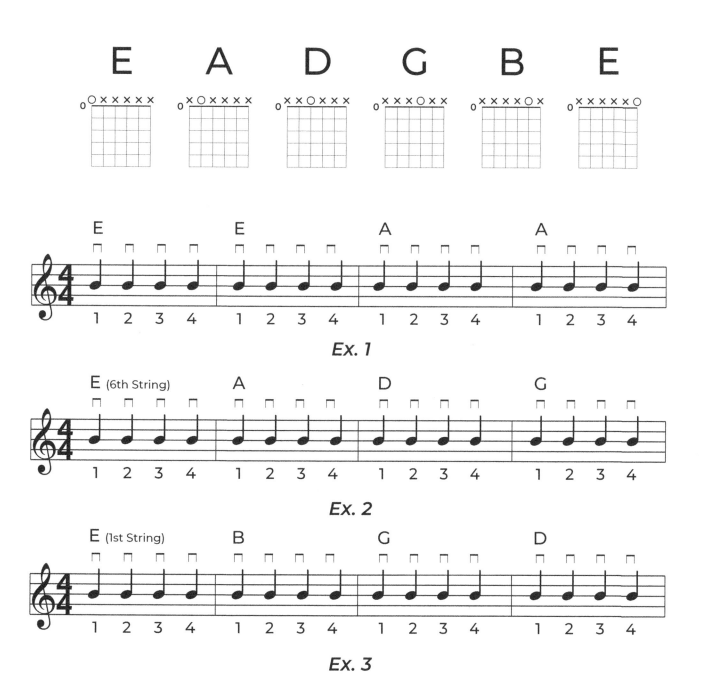

Ex. 1

Ex. 2

Ex. 3

Note: Ordinarily, notes reside on various staff lines, indicating which note is to be played. In this book, the notes just show the rhythm, not the pitch. This is for simplicity while you're first learning.

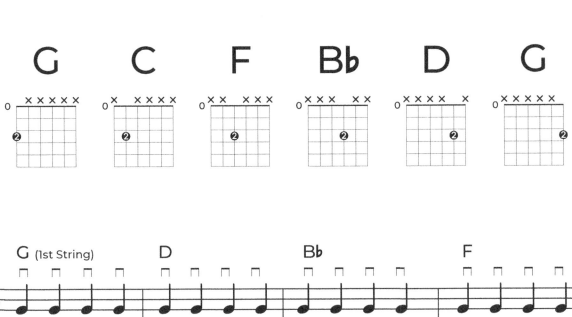

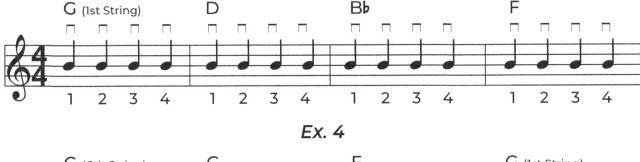

Ex. 4

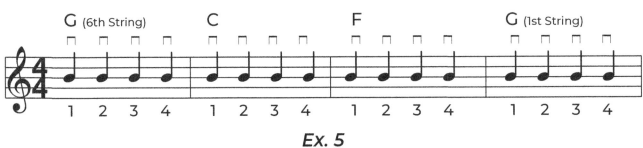

Ex. 5

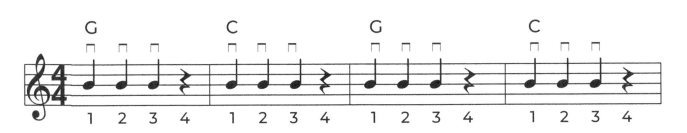

Ex. 6

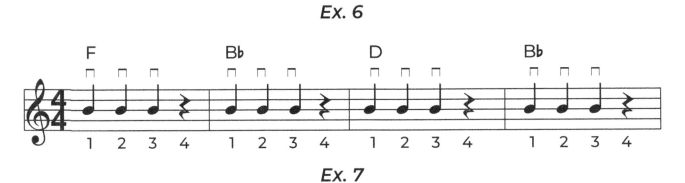

Ex. 7

Mastering Your First Chords: G Major and C Major

TWO OF THE MOST OFTEN PLAYED CHORDS ARE G MAJOR AND C MAJOR. THEY ARE THE ESSENTIAL BUILDING BLOCKS FOR MANY SONGS.

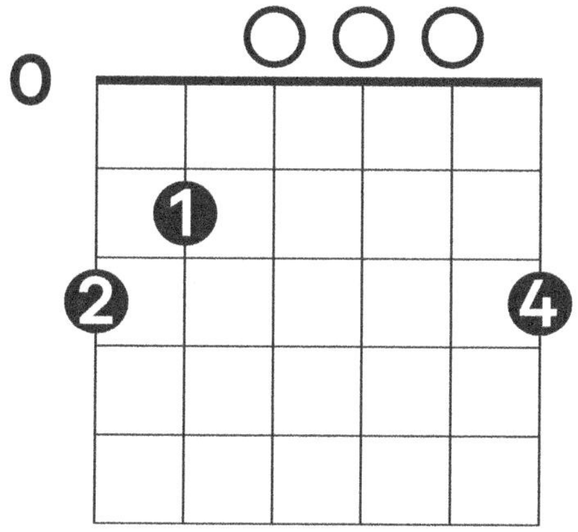

FIG.38 - G MAJOR - FULL

FIG.39 - G MAJOR - FULL HAND POSITION

Notice that the dots on your guitar's neck are at the 3rd and 5th fret. Memorize this. It will come in very handy.

HOW TO PLAY G MAJOR

1 Begin by placing your 2nd finger on the 6th string, 3rd fret. The name of this note is G. It's the root of the G Major chord.

2 Keeping your finger there, add your 1st finger on the 5th string, 2nd fret.

3 The next few strings (4th, 3rd, and 2nd strings) are played open. This means they should ring freely, so be careful not to inadvertently mute them with your fretting hand.

4 Again holding your first two fingers where the are, add your 4th finger on the 1st string, 3rd fret.

5 Strum gently across all the strings, listening for clarity. Adjust your fingers if any note sounds muffled.

6 Repeat this exercise seval times, each time striking one string..at..a..time!

Does this chord seem too difficult right now? Turn the page to find an easier version.

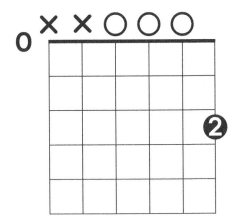

G MAJOR - EASY VERSION

If you've got very small hands, or find the full version of G Major to be too difficult, you can always pull out this awesome one-finger equivalent.

FIG.40 - G MAJOR - EASY

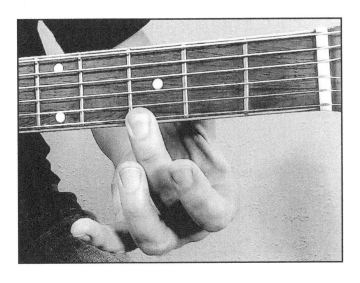

FIG.41 - G MAJOR - EASY HAND POSITION

1 On the 1st string at the 3rd fret, place your 2nd finger Remember to keep it close to the 3rd fret.

2 With your pick or thumb, strum from the 4th string through the 1st. Avoid hitting the 5th and 6th strings.

Exploring G Major

G Major has been a favorite for composers and songwriters alike due to its bright and full-bodied sound.

Congratulations, you just learned your first chord!
G Major is probably the most used of all chords on the acoustic guitar.
You'll be using this chord a lot.

HOW TO PLAY C MAJOR

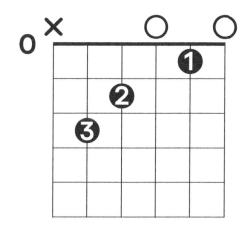

1 Begin by pressing down on the 5th string, 3rd fret with your 3rd finger. This note is C, the root of C Major.

2 On the 4th string at the 2nd fret, add your 2nd finger.

3 Let the 3rd string ring open - no fingers needed here!

4 On the 2nd string at the 1st fret, place your 1st finger.

5 Ensure the 1st string is played open, allowing it to resonate clearly. Check to make sure your 1st finger is bent up and over this string.

FIG.42 - C MAJOR - FULL

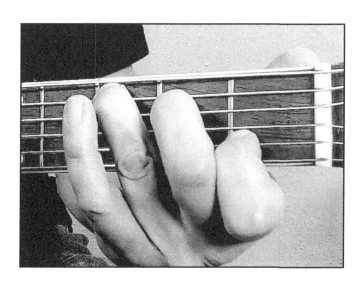

FIG.43 - C MAJOR - FULL HAND POSITION

When playing C Major, the 6th string isn't used. Be careful to not accidentally strum it. This takes practice.

How Guitar Became a Mainstay in Popular Music

The guitar became prominent in popular music in the 1950s with the rise of rock 'n' roll.

C MAJOR - EASY VERSION

One of the great things about the guitar is that there are **lots and lots** of ways to play any chord! Here's a super-simple version of C Major.

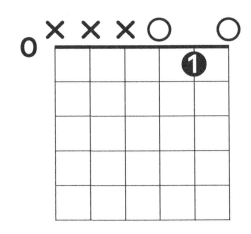

Fig.44 - C Major - Easy

1 On the 2nd string at the 1st fret, place your 1st finger. Remember to keep it close to the 1st fret.

2 With your pick or thumb, strum the 3rd, 2nd and 1st strings. Avoid hitting the 4th, 5th and 6th strings.

And that's it! A super-simple, one-note C Major that sounds great, too.

G Major and C Major sound terrific together, which is why they're found in so many songs.

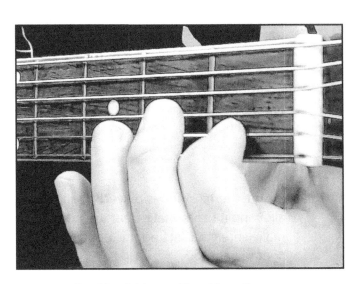

Fig.45 - C Major - Easy Hand Position

TROUBLESHOOT YOUR FRETTING HAND

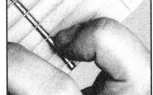

GETTING STUCK? HERE'S HOW TO IMPROVE YOUR TECHNIQUE.

Watch your finger posture. Your fingertips should be almost perpendicular to the fretboard, not slanting or resting lazily. Guitar strings are pretty close together and it's easy to accidentally touch two strings with the same finger.

Keep your fingers very close to the frets. This takes a little experimentation. Keeping your fingers near the frets improves the sustain and tone of the note.

How to find the problem finger: Starting with the lowest string of your chord, pick each string slowly and one-at-a-time. If your fret hand is in the correct position, you'll each each note ring clearly without stopping early, sounding muted or buzzing.

EXERCISES FOR G AND C CHORDS

NOW THAT YOU'VE LEARNED THE BASICS, IT'S TIME TO CONNECT THE CHORDS AND PLAY SOME MUSIC!

In the following progressions, you'll read from left-to-right. Each chord should be played four times as indicated by the music notes. Play very slowly at first and keep your eye on the changing chord name.

In the 4th example, the new symbol is a quarter-rest. Like a quarternote, it also has a one-count length, but it is silent, not strummed.

(Note: If you're used to reading music, discregard the note of the staff on which the notes sit. They just mark when to play the given chords.)

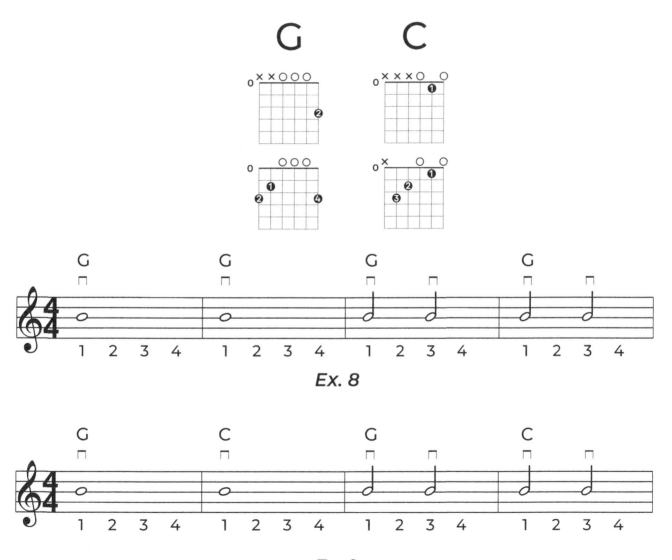

Ex. 8

Ex. 9

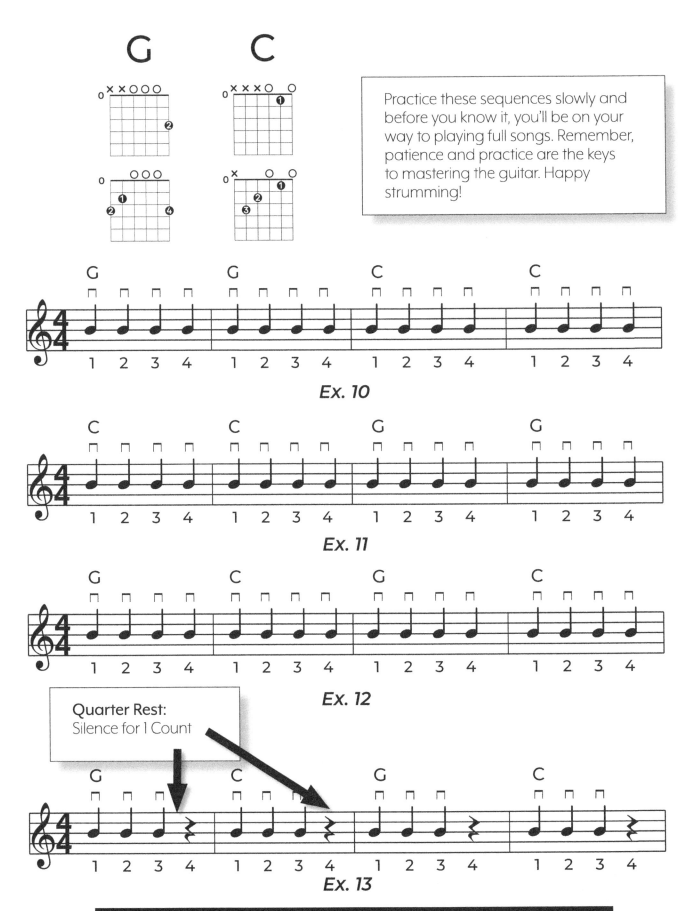

Practice these sequences slowly and before you know it, you'll be on your way to playing full songs. Remember, patience and practice are the keys to mastering the guitar. Happy strumming!

Ex. 10

Ex. 11

Ex. 12

Quarter Rest: Silence for 1 Count

Ex. 13

How do these chords feel? Difficult? Strange? Like you need longer fingers? Every student feels this way at first. With practice, it gets much easier.

Essential Knowledge: D Major

D MAJOR IS AN ESSENTIAL CHORD FOR GUITARISTS. USED UNIVERSALLY, IT HAS A UNIQUE PLACE IN EVERY GUITARIST'S TOOLKIT.

HOW TO PLAY D MAJOR USING 3 FINGERS

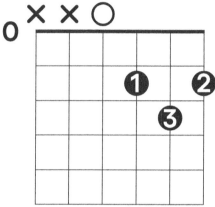

Fig.46 - D Major - Full

Begin by studying the D Major chord. You'll see that its root note is the open 4th string, which is D.

1 Start your finger placements with your 1st finger on the 2nd fret of the 3rd string.

2 Next, place your 3rd finger on the 3rd fret of the 2nd string.

3 Complete the chord by placing your 2nd finger on the 2nd fret of the 1st string.

4 When you strum, ensure you only play strings 1 through 4, avoiding the 6th and 5th strings to maintain the chord's integrity.

Fig.47 - D Major - Full Hand Position

When compared to many of the chords you'll learn in this book, D Major sounds a little less full and has a little less volume. That's because it doesn't use the 5th or 6th strings which are more bass-heavy. That's not bad, it just makes D Major a little different.

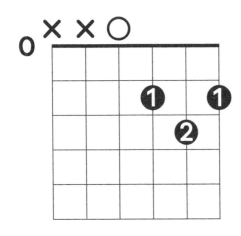

FIG.49 - D MAJOR - BARRE VERSION

D MAJOR - BARRE VERSION

Many students find the conventional way of playing D Major with three fingers to be very difficult. Another way only uses two fingers. Depending on your personal preference, this may be an easier way. Use whichever method you prefer.

1 Play the open 4th string, D.

2 Place your 1st finger on the 2nd fret of the 3rd String.

3 Add your 2nd finger on the 3rd fret of the 2nd string.

FIG.48 - D MAJOR - BARRE HAND POSITION

4 Lay your 1st finger across all three strings, 1 through 3. The tip will remain on the 2nd string and the middle part of your finger will depress the 1st string at the 2nd fret.

Throughout this book, the traditional chord fingering is referred to often. However, feel free to use whichever D Major chord fingering you find easier and more comfortable.

5 When you strum, ensure you only play strings 1 through 4, avoiding the 6th and 5th strings.

D MAJOR - EASY VERSION

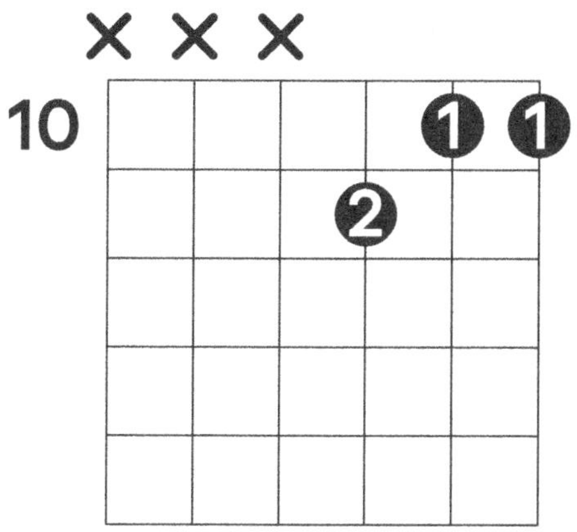

10 × × ×

Fig.50 - D Major - Easy

1 The number "10" in this chord diagram lets you know it is way up the neck. Ready to go? First, find your 10th fret.

2 Start your finger placement with your 2nd finger. On the 3rd string, at the 11th fret, hold it down now.

Fig.51 - D Major - Easy Hand Position

3 Next, put your 1st finger tip on the 2nd string at the 10th fret. Roll it down, so it's barre holding down both the 2nd and 1st strings.

4 When you strum, only play strings 3 through 1, avoiding the 4th, 5th and 6th strings.

Everyone Loves D Major!

D Major is known for its bright and triumphant sound.

The Origins of the Fretboard

The fretboard with raised frets is believed to have originated in the Middle East before spreading to Europe.

EXERCISES FOR D MAJOR

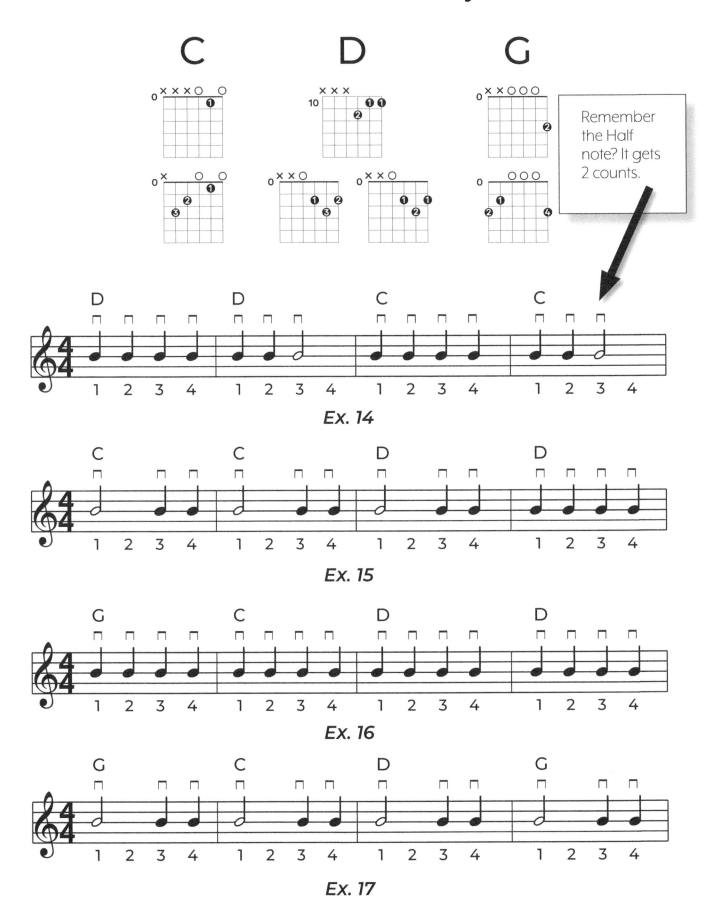

Ex. 14

Ex. 15

Ex. 16

Ex. 17

Basic Strumming

THE 3 PARTS OF MUSIC ARE MELODY, HARMONY OR RHYTHM. STRUMMING ADDS RHYTHM AND AN OPPORTUNITY FOR VARIETY.

STRUMMING BASICS: JUST DOWN AND UP

Strumming involves two fundamental motions: the downstroke and the upstroke. Think of it as a continuous loop; for every downstroke, there will be a subsequent upstroke to bring your hand back to the starting point.

Start by practicing this motion without producing any sound. Simply move your strumming hand in a down, up pattern above the strings without making contact. This helps you get accustomed to the rhythm and movement.

FIG.52 - DOWNSTROKE

FIG.53 - UPSTROKE

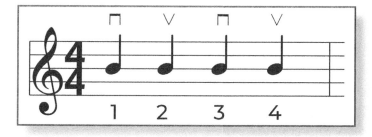

These marks indicate a Downstroke on beats 1 and 3, Upstroke on 2 and 4.

They read: "Down, Up, Down, Up."

STRUMMING WORKSHOP: G MAJOR

GRAB A METRONOME AND SET IT TO 50 BPM FOR THIS RHYTHM-BUILDING WORKOUT. USE EITHER OF THE G MAJOR CHORDS BELOW.

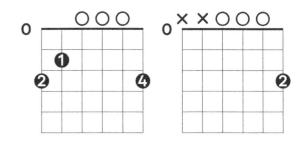

1 Strum the pattern shown. On every count of "1" and "3", you'll strum downward (toward the floor) and on "2" and "4", you'll strum the strings upward, as shown by the down- and upstroke marks over each beat.

2 Now switch to downstrokes on all four beats.

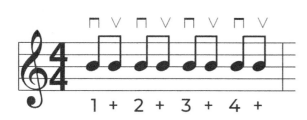

3 Add the upstrokes. These are eighth-notes, counted "One, -and, Two, -and..." Strum downward on the beat, upward on the "-and".

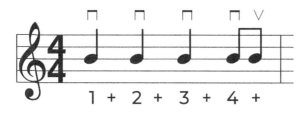

4 Put it all together for this combo rhythm! Use downstrokes on beats 1, 2 and 3. Play the fourth beat with a downstroke and upstroke on the "-and".

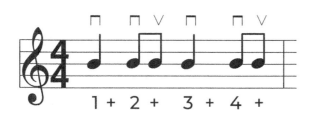

5 One more combo: Downstrokes on beats "1" and "3", down- and up- on "2 +" and "4 +".

Strumming adds rhythm and energy to your music. Rhythm adds variety and keeps things interesting.

Next, position your left hand to play an E Major chord.

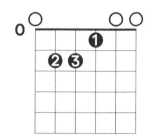 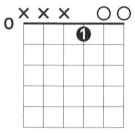

E Major Chords

With this chord held down, try the eighth-note strumming pattern, emphasizing both the down and up movements equally.

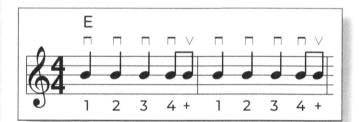

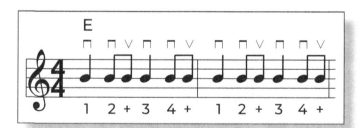

This rhythm you're practicing is based on eighth-notes. Two eighth-notes combined equal to one quarter-note.

From Elvis to Ed Sheeran: The Evolution of Strumming Patterns

Strumming patterns have evolved with music styles, from the straight-ahead patterns of rock 'n' roll to the more complex syncopated patterns of modern pop.

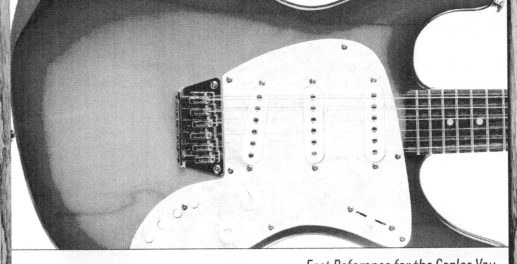

Big Open Chords: E Major and A Major

ANOTHER PAIR OF COMMON CHORDS IS THE DYNAMIC DUO OF E MAJOR AND A MAJOR. THESE CHORDS NOT ONLY RESONATE BEAUTIFULLY BUT ARE BUILDING BLOCKS FOR MANY POPULAR SONGS.

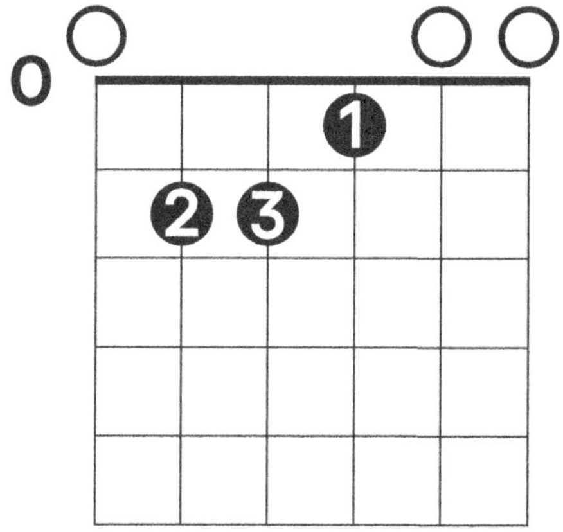

HOW TO PLAY E MAJOR

1 Start with the 6th string - it's played open, which means no fret fingers are needed.

2 Next, on the 5th string, position your 2nd finger on the 2nd fret.

3 Now on the 4th string at the 2nd fret, add your 3rd finger.

4 On the 3rd string at the 1st fret, add your 1st finger.

5 Now, maintain an arch in your hand to ensure the 2nd and 1st strings remain untouched, allowing them to ring out clearly when strummed.

6 Now, confidently strum all six strings. Ensure each note resonates clearly. If you encounter muffled notes or buzzing strings, adjust your hand positioning slightly and ensure your fingertips are close to the frets.

FIG.54 - E MAJOR - FULL

FIG.55 - E MAJOR - FULL - HAND POSITION

E MAJOR - EASY VERSION

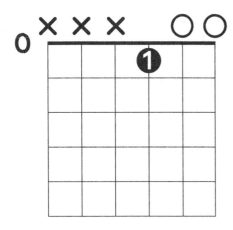

FIG.56 - E MAJOR - EASY

Here's a pretty little chord and a super-easy way to play E Major.

1 On the 3rd string at the 1st fret, place your 1st finger.

FIG.57 - E MAJOR - EASY HAND POSITION

2 Strum from the 3rd string through the 1st. Avoid hitting the 4th, 5th or 6th strings.

Acoustic Guitar for Adults

HOW TO PLAY A MAJOR

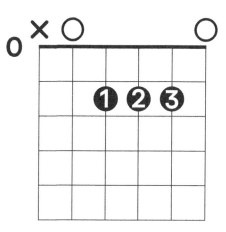

1 Notice that the 6th string isn't used in this A Major chord. The 6th string has an "X" over it. So, begin with the 5th string played open. This is the open A-string.

2 On the 4th string at the 2nd fret, place your 1st finger.

Fig.58 - A Major - Full

3 While holding that note, you're going to add two more fingers to the next strings, all on the same fret, the 2nd fret. Add your 2nd finger to the 3rd string and your 3rd finger to the 2nd string.

4 Ensure your hand has a slight arch, letting the 1st string sound freely. The arch gets your fingers around the neck, around the fretboard and over the 1st string which you shouldn't touch.

5 Strum the first five strings, checking for clarity in each note. Adjust your positioning if necessary until each note sounds distinct.

Fig.59 - A Major - Full - Hand Position

Bob Marley: The Acoustic Side

Bob Marley is known for reggae and his electric performances, but his acoustic renditions showcase the versatility and depth of his songwriting.

A MAJOR - EASY VERSION

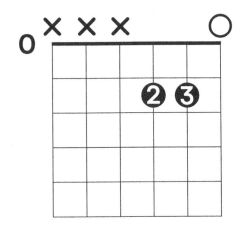

FIG.60 - A MAJOR - EASY

1 On the 3rd string at the 2nd fret, place your 2nd finger. Remember to keep it close to the 2nd fret.

2 Keeping that finger there, add the 3rd string at the 2nd fret, using your 3rd finger.

3 With your pick or thumb, strum just the 3rd, 2nd and 1st strings.

FIG.61 - A MAJOR - EASY - HAND POSITION

YOU'VE BEEN INTRODUCED TO QUARTER-NOTES PREVIOUSLY. NOW EXPLORE SOME RHYTHMS THAT MERGE QUARTER-NOTES WITH HALF-NOTES.

RHYTHMIC EXERCISES

A half-note is equivalent to the duration of two quarter-notes. Count aloud: "One, Two, Three, Four". Here, each word signifies a quarter-note, while a half-note would span two counts, like "One, Two" or "Three, Four".

Try out these rhythmic patterns using the chords shown.

Listening to your progress, you're undoubtedly crafting melodies. A round of applause is in order: you're not just playing notes; you're making music! Celebrate your achievements, musician!

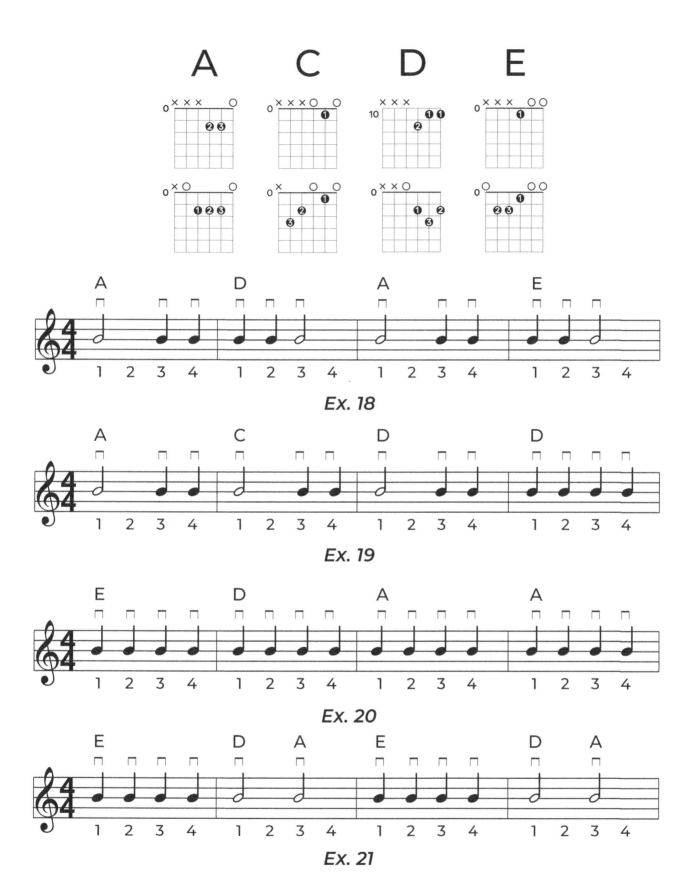

Ex. 18

Ex. 19

Ex. 20

Ex. 21

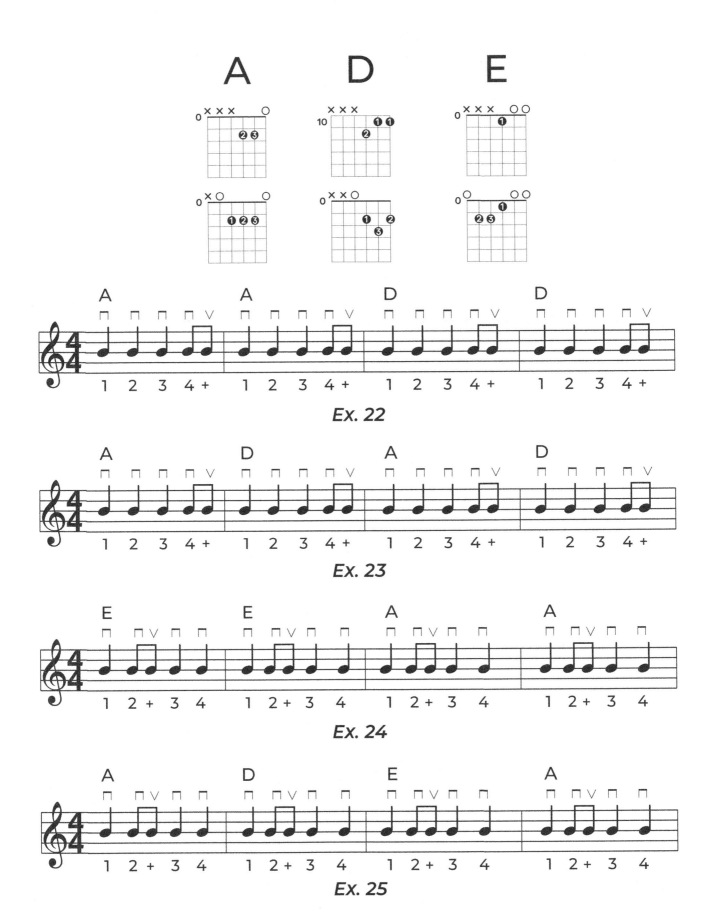

Ex. 22

Ex. 23

Ex. 24

Ex. 25

Learn Minor Chords: E and A Minor

WAIT, DIDN'T YOU JUST LEARN THESE CHORDS? WELL NOT QUITE, BUT NOW THAT YOU KNOW E AND A MAJOR, YOU'LL REALLY ENJOY LEARNING THEIR MINOR COUNTERPARTS.

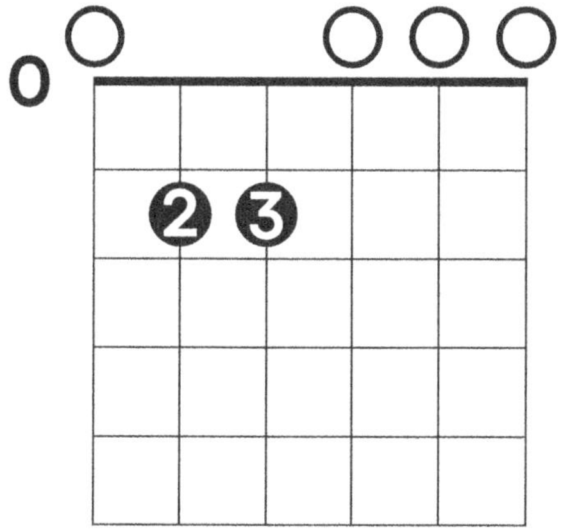

HOW TO PLAY E MINOR

1 You're going to recognize many of these notes from E Major. Start with the open-6th string. Play it without a fretting finger.

2 Next, on the 5th string at the 2nd fret, position your 2nd finger.

3 At the 4th string, 2nd fret, add your 3rd finger.

4 Maintain an arch in your hand to ensure the 3rd, 2nd and 1st strings remain untouched, allowing them to ring out clearly when strummed.

5 Now, give a strum to all six strings and hear the big, rich sound.

Fig.62 - E Minor - Full

Fig.63 - E Minor - Full Hand Position

The Versatility of E Minor

Big and beautiful, E Minor is a versatile chord, fitting seamlessly into genres ranging from classical to heavy metal.

Minor chords tend to sound sad, where Major sounds happy.

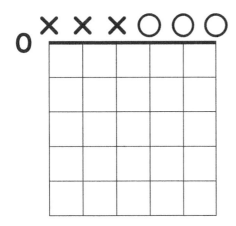

FIG.64 - E MINOR - EASY

FIG.65 - E MINOR - EASY HAND POSITION

E MINOR - EASY VERSION

How about a chord that doesn't require any fingers? Sounds good!

1 Strum from the 3rd string through the 1st, just those three strings. Just one step: That's it!

HOW TO PLAY A MINOR

1 Just like A Major, the 6th string isn't involved in the A Minor chord. The 6th string has an "X" over it. So, begin with the 5th string played open.

2 On the 4th string at the 2nd fret, place your 2nd finger.

3 While holding that note, on the 3rd string at the 2nd fret add your 3rd finger and on the 2nd string at the 1st fret, add your 1st finger.

4 Ensure your hand has a slight arch, letting the 1st string sound freely.

5 Give your A Minor chord a strum. Does each note sound approximately the same volume? Did you remember to not hit the 6th string?

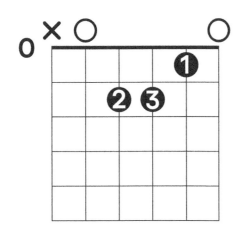

FIG.66 - A MINOR - FULL

FIG.67 - A MINOR - FULL HAND POSITION

A MINOR - EASY VERSION

1 On the 3rd string at the 2nd fret, place your 2nd finger. Remember to keep it close to the 2nd fret.

2 Keeping that finger there, add the 2nd string at the 1st fret, using your 1st finger.

3 With your pick or thumb, strum just the 3rd through 1st strings.

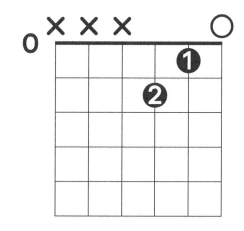

FIG.68 - A MINOR - EASY

FIG.69 - A MINOR - EASY HAND POSITION

A Minor's Melancholic Beauty

A Minor is often associated with a somber and reflective mood in music, making it a go-to key for emotional songs.

Women Guitarists Who Shaped Music

Pioneering women like Memphis Minnie and Maybelle Carter played pivotal roles in the development of blues and country guitar styles.

Today, classical guitarist Sharon Isbin is regarded as one of the very best to have ever played the instrument.

EXERCISES FOR A MINOR AND E MINOR

Ex. 26

Ex. 27

Ex. 28

Ex. 29

You've already learned a LOT of chords and rhythms.
Whenever learning new music, take the time to slow down the tempo.
Slowing down makes it easier to play correctly. Speed will come later.

Ex. 30

Ex. 31

Ex. 32

Ex. 33

Ex. 34

Ex. 35

Ex. 36

Ex. 37

Chords Going Up the Fretboard: F Major and B-flat Major

F AND B-FLAT MAJOR ARE USED IN LOTS OF PIANO-DRIVEN SONGS. MOST STUDENTS FIND THESE CHORDS CHALLENGING TO PLAY AT FIRST, BUT EASIER WITH PRACTICE.

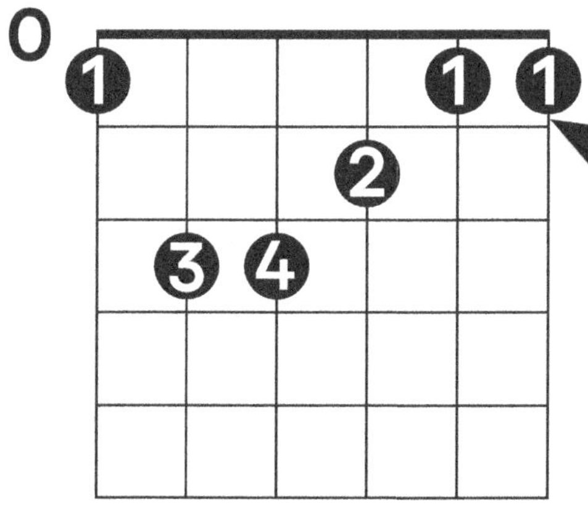

HOW TO PLAY F MAJOR

1 Begin on the 6th string at the 1st fret. Place your 1st finger. Remember to keep your finger close to the 1st fret.

> Your 1st finger will fret 3 different strings in this barre chord.

2 Lay your finger down on the fretboard like a log on train tracks. Your finger will be so nearly flat that you will also fret the 1st and 2nd strings with your 1st finger.

3 With your 1st finger now in place, begin adding your remaining fingers. On the 5th string at the 3rd fret, add your 3rd finger.

4 Next on the 4th string, 3rd fret, add your 4th finger.

5 Lastly, to the 3rd string, 2nd fret add your 2nd finger.

6 Strum gently across all the strings, listening for clarity. Adjust your fingers if any note sounds muffled.

7 Repeat this exercise seval times, each time striking one string..at..a..time!

FIG.70 - F MAJOR - FULL

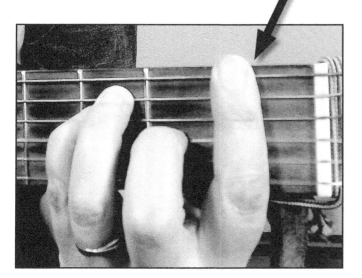

FIG.71 - F MAJOR - FULL - HAND POSITION

Reaching for that low F takes a lot of strength, but mostly great hand position. If you're having difficulty, check your arm, wrist and hand alignment.

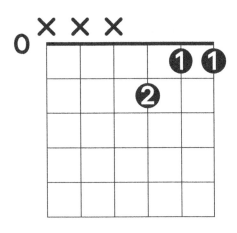

F MAJOR - EASY VERSION

Fig.72 - F Major - Easy

1 On the 2nd string at the 1st fret, add your 1st finger. Keep your fingertip there, but roll your finger down slightly so you're also fretting the 1st string.

2 On the 3rd string at the 2nd fret, add your 2nd finger.

3 With your pick or thumb, strum 3rd, 2nd and 1st strings. Avoid hitting the other strings.

Why F Major Challenges Beginners

The F Major chord can be a hurdle due to its barre requirement; building hand strength and proper technique is key.

Fig.73 - F Major - Easy Hand Position

Acoustic Guitar for Adults

HOW TO PLAY B-FLAT MAJOR

1 Begin at the 5th string, 1st fret with your 1st finger. This is B-flat, the root of B-flat Major.

2 On the 4th string at the 3rd fret, add your 2nd finger.

3 Now keeping your fingertip there, roll your 4th finger downward until it is also fretting the 3rd and 2nd strings.

4 Strum the 5th, 4th, 3rd and 2nd strings only, avoiding the 6th and 1st.

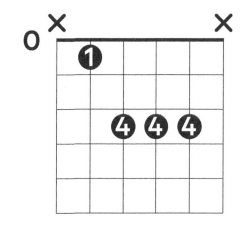

FIG.74 - B-FLAT MAJOR - FULL

FIG.75 - B-FLAT MAJOR - FULL HAND POSITION

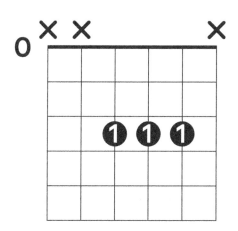

FIG.76 - B-FLAT MAJOR - EASY

FIG.77 - B-FLAT MAJOR - EASY HAND POSITION

B-FLAT MAJOR - EASY VERSION

1 Begin at the 4th string, 3rd fret with your 1st finger.

2 Keeping your fingertip there, roll your 1st finger downward until it is also fretting the 3rd and 2nd strings.

3 Strum the 4th, 3rd and 2nd strings only, avoiding the others.

CHORDS GOING UP THE FRETBOARD

Until now, every chord you've learned has been played very near the nut. You know they're near the nut because each chord diagram has a "0" in the upper corner, near the thick line indicating the nut of the guitar. Both features tell you that the chord diagram is describing that part of the fretboard.

But what about chords in the middle of the neck? Or even higher? What do those chord diagrams look like?

Equivalent Chords - Different Notations

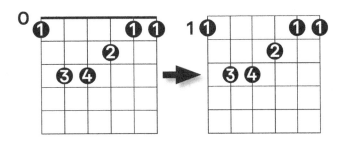

You already know that chord diagrams tell you which fingers to use, and where to place them. Until now, every chord has been near the nut, indicated by the "0" in the upper-corner. But what if that "0" were some other number? How should you read and play it?

The number in the upper-corner is the **Origin Fret Number**. It tells you where the diagram starts on the fretboard.

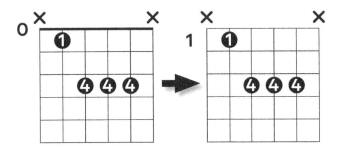

Study the two diagrams for F Major at left. In this chapter, you learned the one on the left, with the Origin Fret "0". You know that the black dots with the number "1" mean you place your first finger on the first fret.

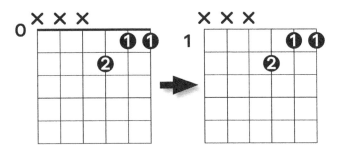

The equivalent diagram on the right shows the same thing, but instead of a fret origin of "0", it is a "1". That "1" means the 1st fret in the diagram is the 1st fret on your guitar.

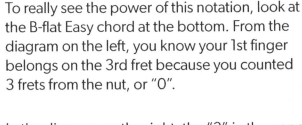

To really see the power of this notation, look at the B-flat Easy chord at the bottom. From the diagram on the left, you know your 1st finger belongs on the 3rd fret because you counted 3 frets from the nut, or "0".

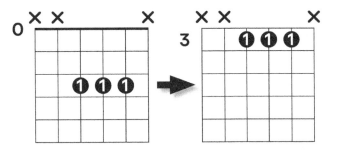

In the diagram on the right, the "3" in the upper-corner means the first fret of that diagram is the 3rd fret on your guitar. They are the same chord, but the version on the right is the more common way to write it.

FIG. 78 - EQUIVALENT CHORD NOTATIONS

EXERCISES FOR F AND B-FLAT CHORDS

Rhythm Builder: *The Tie* Notice how there is a curved line connecting beats 2 and 3 in these exercises? That curve is called a *Tie* and it tells you to hold the note from the first beat through the second. You'll strike the note on beat 2 and let it ring through beat 3 without striking it again. It gets plucked once, but held for two beats.

Ex. 38

Ex. 39

Ex. 40

Ex. 41

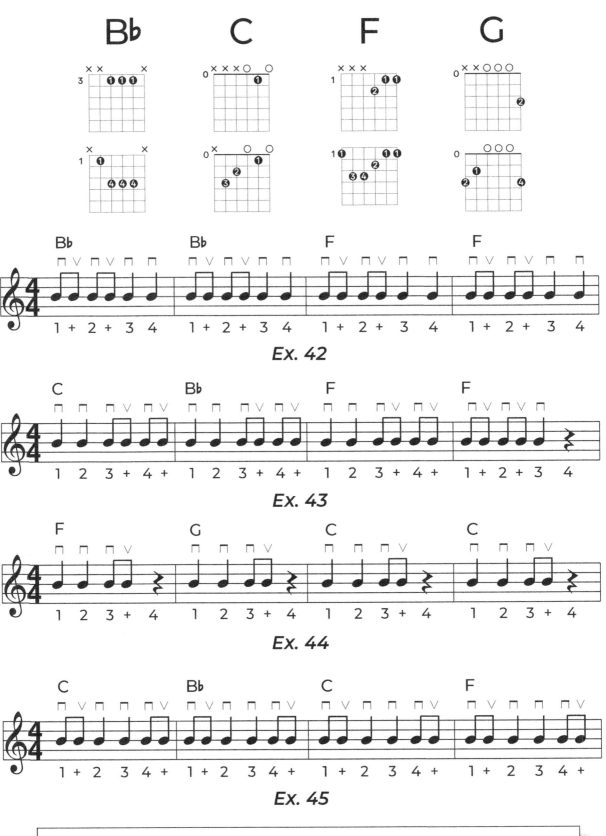

Ex. 42

Ex. 43

Ex. 44

Ex. 45

Practice these sequences with their various rhythms and before you know it, you'll be on your way to playing full songs. Remember patience, practice and persistence are the keys to mastering the guitar.

TAKE AN IN-DEPTH LOOK AT THE MECHANICS OF MAJOR BARRE CHORDS AND EXPLORE THEIR VISUAL SYMMETRY ACROSS THE FRETBOARD.

5TH-STRING MAJOR BARRE CHORDS

Chances are, you've heard of barre chords, but what are they?

Barre chords are some of the most useful in all of guitar playing. The "barre" uses one finger to press down on multiple strings simultaneously. Examine these two versions of the A Major chord:

* Seen here, the traditional A Major chord using 3 fingers, where each note is played with a different finger.

* And, here is the barre chord version of A Major. Notice that both the 1st and 6th strings are not played.

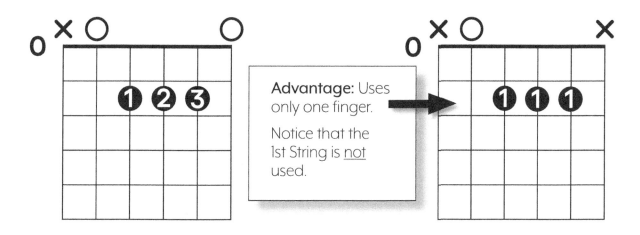

Advantage: Uses only one finger.

Notice that the 1st String is <u>not</u> used.

FIG.79 - A MAJOR   FIG.80 - A MAJOR BARRE

In the barre chord version, the open 1st string isn't played. Yet, the chord retains its robust and full sound. Notice how the barre chord uses only one finger, the 1st finger. It's easy to play, easy to remember and sounds great, too.

Why barre chords are important: Often, the same chord "shape" can be moved up and down the neck to instantly create new chords. Much easier than remembering a new chord shape for every chord, one chord shape can be used all over the place!

How to Play: A Major Barre

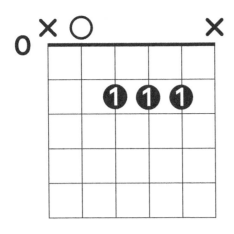

FIG.81 - A MAJOR BARRE

1 Start by positioning the tip of your 1st finger on the 2nd fret of the 4th string and play that note.

2 Now, envision your 1st finger as a log laid across train tracks. Roll this finger downwards, making it lie flat across the adjacent strings.

3 Strum the three fretted notes. Now, play them individually to ensure your fretting hand is positioned optimally.

4 Have a listen to your barre chord. Strum those four strings while being mindful to avoid both the 1st and 6th strings.

FIG.82 - A MAJOR BARRE - HAND POSITION

Adapting to the barre technique can feel unfamiliar at first. However, with regular practice, you'll begin to refine your finger positioning, making it feel much more natural and making it sound better, too.

Move It Up: B Major Barre

1 Beginning with the 5th string at the 2nd fret, place your 1st finger. This note is B, the root note of the chord. Play it to make sure it sounds good.

2 Now, position the tip of your 4th finger on the 4th string at the 4th fret and play that note.

3 Proceed to roll this finger downwards, letting it rest across the 3rd and 2nd strings, as well.

4 Take care to not strum the 6th or 1st strings.

SEEING MUSIC

This book is published by Seeing Music. The idea of "seeing" music comes from the visual aspect of learning and mastering guitar. Observing the fretboard patterns of the A Major and B Major barre chords reveals their striking resemblance. This symmetry is not limited to these two chords alone. As you progress up the guitar's neck, you'll encounter numerous barre chords resembling the B Major chord's pattern. Recognizing these visual patterns can really speed your learning curve.

In essence, barre chords are not just about finger strength or positioning but also about visual recognition. Understanding these patterns ensures you're well-equipped to seamlessly navigate the vast ocean of major barre chords that are waiting ahead!

This is the more common way this chord is drawn.

This is the same B Major barre chord as above. All that has changed is the number in the upper-left corner, indicating that your first finger is placed at the 2nd fret.

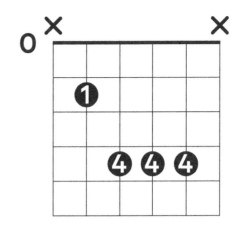

FIG.83 - B MAJOR BARRE

FIG.84 - B MAJOR BARRE - HAND POSITION

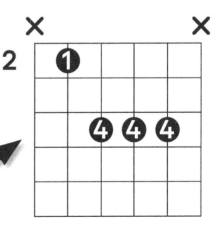

FIG.85 - B MAJOR BARRE

Move It Up: C Major Barre

1 Begin with the 5th string at the 3rd fret. Place your 1st finger here. This is C, the root of the chord. Play it to make sure it sounds good.

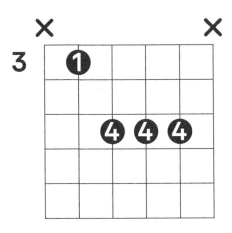

FIG.86 - C MAJOR BARRE

2 Now, position the tip of your 4th finger on the 4th string at the 5th fret and play that note.

3 Proceed to roll this finger downwards, letting it rest across the 3rd and 2nd strings, as well.

FIG.87 - C MAJOR BARRE - EASY HAND POSITION

The Beatles and the Barre Chord Revolution

The Beatles' use of barre chords in their music helped popularize these forms among aspiring guitarists.

Here's another way to think about it:

Move the B Major Barre chord up the neck one fret. The lowest note, played by your 1st finger should be on the 5th string, 3rd fret. Two frets higher, you'll place your 4th finger in a barre across strings 4, 3 and 2.

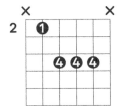

Move each note of B Major up one fret to become C Major

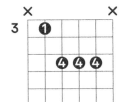

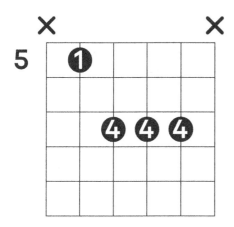

×   ×

5   ❶

❹ ❹ ❹

FIG.88 - D MAJOR BARRE

Move It Up Again: D Major Barre

1 Just as before, begin on the 5th string, this time at the 5th fret and place your 1st finger. This is D.

2 Again, add your 4th finger across all three strings, 4, 3 and 2, now at the 7th fret. Give your chord a strum.

FIG.89 - D MAJOR BARRE - HAND POSITION

Are you seeing the similarities between these chords? How about the sound? Can you hear the similarites between them?

Isn't this fun? With the same chord shape, you can make many different chords, just by moving up the neck. Look at all the barre chords you know:

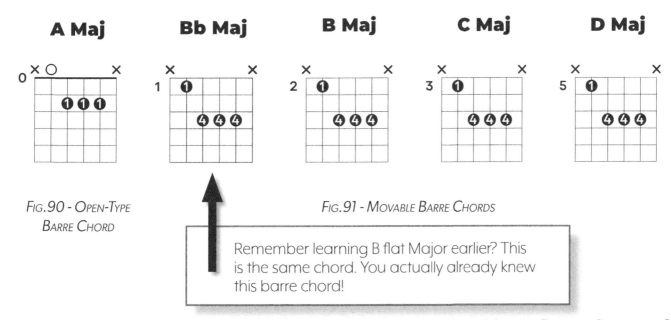

A Maj   **Bb Maj**   **B Maj**   **C Maj**   **D Maj**

FIG.90 - OPEN-TYPE BARRE CHORD

FIG.91 - MOVABLE BARRE CHORDS

Remember learning B flat Major earlier? This is the same chord. You actually already knew this barre chord!

Ask a Pro: Barre Chords make it so easy to move the same chord shape up and down the neck. So why should I learn the other basic chord shapes? Like the ones that use open-strings?

The short answer is: Because they sound different.

One very unique and awesome thing about the guitar is that the same notes and chords can be found in many places, played many ways. Each placement or chord fingering has a different sound from every other. Chords using open-strings have a ringing, bell-like quality. Barre chords sound a little more powerful and punchy. Both are good, but different.

Music is art and artists need to be creative. Depending on the type of music and style you'll be playing, you may prefer one type of chord to another at a given point in the song. Also, you may learn some different picking techniques that lend themselves to either open-string chords or barre chords.

Learning Bonus: Explore Your Fingerboard

To see an example of how the same note is usually found in many places around the fingerboard, try this exercise:

1 Play the 1st string, open E.

2 Now play the note on the 2nd string at the 5th fret, which is also E. Notice how they are the same pitch?

3 On the 3rd string at the 9th fret, play this E.

4 Moving up the neck again, on the 4th string at the 14th fret, play the same note, E.

All of these are the same pitch. Play them again and notice the difference in tone between them. The brightest sounding tone is found with the open E. The 14th fret sounds more round. Would you agree?

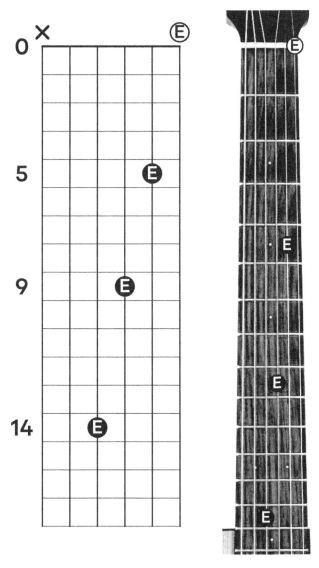

FIG.92 - EQUIVALENT NOTES ON THE FRETBOARD

This is one of the things that make stringed instruments like the guitar so special: Guitarists have options for where to play a note (Think of the piano: Each note has only one key, in just one location.) This gives the player some freedom to flow chords and melodies together. It also gives tonal options which make the guitar such an expressive instrument.

6TH-STRING MAJOR BARRE CHORDS

AS YOU COULD PROBABLY GUESS, 6TH-STRING BARRE CHORDS HAVE THEIR LOWEST NOTE ON THE 6TH-STRING.

Remember that barre chords can be moved up and down the neck to instantly create new chords. There are two basic types and you've already learned 5th-String Barre Chords.

You've also learned that notes and chords can be played in a variety of ways around the guitar fretboard. So, here's yet another way to play A Major, using a 6th-String Barre Chord.

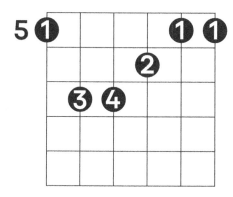

FIG.93 - A MAJOR BARRE

How to Play 6th-String A Major Barre

1 Start on the 6th string at the 5th fret. Place your 1st finger there.

2 Now, envision your 1st finger as a log laid across train tracks. Roll this finger downwards, making it lie flat across the adjacent strings.

3 Now add your 3rd, 4th then 2nd fingers as in the diagram.

4 Strum all 6 notes. Now, play them individually to ensure your fretting hand is positioned optimally. Listen for buzzes or bad notes and adjust your fingers slightly to improve your tone.

FIG.94 - A MAJOR BARRE - HAND POSITION

Notice how the guitarist's thumb is out-of-sight in the A Major Barre photo above. That's a key point, enabling the player to comfortably reach all those notes.

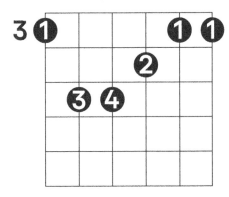

Fig.95 - G Major Barre

Move it Down: G Major Barre

1 Start on the 6th string at the 3rd fret. Place your 1st finger there.

2 Now, lay your 1st finger across the fretboard. As you roll this finger downwards, make it lie flat across the adjacent strings.

3 Now add your 3rd, 4th then 2nd fingers as in the diagram.

Fig.96 - G Major Barre - Hand Position

Now Move It Up, Up, Up: B Major Barre

1 Just as with A Major and G Major Barres, You'll place your 1st finger across the fretboard, then add your other fingers.

2 B Major begins with your 1st finger on the 6th string at the 7th fret. Now, roll it across all 6 strings so it's ready to play the three strings shown in the diagram.

3 Place the remainder of your fingers: 3, 4 and then 2.

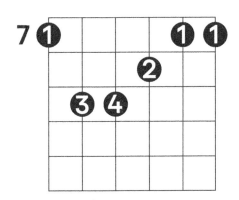

Fig.97 - B Major Barre

Fig.98 - B Major Barre - Hand Position

6th-Type Major Barre Chords

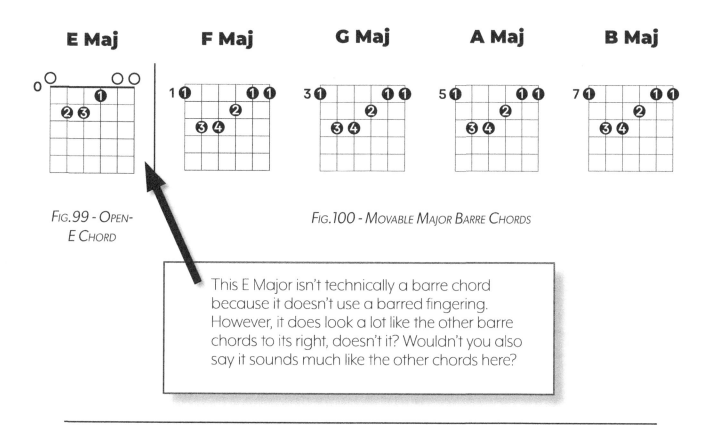

E Maj   F Maj   G Maj   A Maj   B Maj

FIG.99 - OPEN-E CHORD

FIG.100 - MOVABLE MAJOR BARRE CHORDS

This E Major isn't technically a barre chord because it doesn't use a barred fingering. However, it does look a lot like the other barre chords to its right, doesn't it? Wouldn't you also say it sounds much like the other chords here?

5th-Type Major Barre Chords

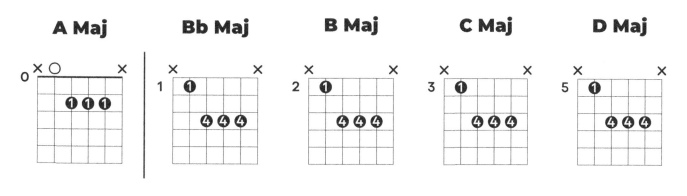

A Maj   Bb Maj   B Maj   C Maj   D Maj

FIG.101 - OPEN-TYPE BARRE CHORD

FIG.102 - MOVABLE MAJOR BARRE CHORDS

Open-String Chords

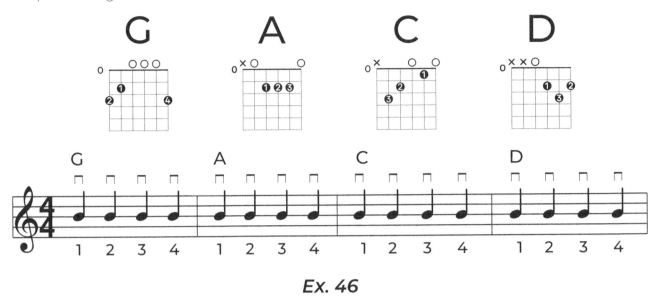

Ex. 46

Barre Chords

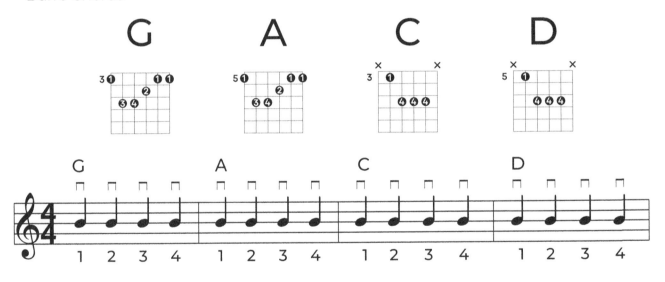

Ex. 47

Open-string chords and barre chords sound different.

To compare, play the open-string versions in the first exercise, then the next using only barre-chords.

Open-String Chords

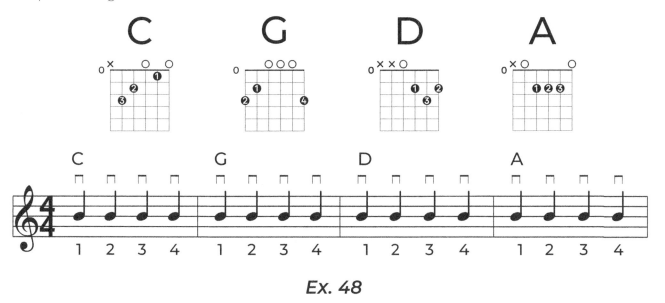

Ex. 48

Barre Chords

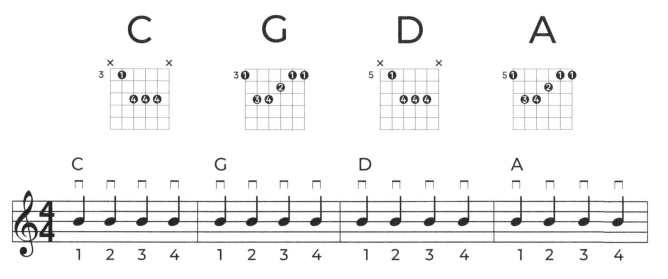

Ex. 49

Moving Chords: Minor Barre Chords

MINOR BARRE CHORDS ARE THE MINOR VERSION OF MAJOR BARRE CHORDS. JUST LIKE THEIR MAJOR CHORD RELATIVES, THEY ALSO MAKE IT EASY TO PLAY CHORDS UP AND DOWN THE NECK.

5TH STRING MINOR BARRE CHORDS

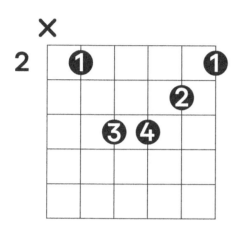

FIG.103 - B MINOR BARRE

How to Play B Minor Barre

1 Start on the 5th string at the 2nd fret and position the tip of your 1st finger near the fret.

2 Now, lay your 1st finger across the adjacent strings.

3 Continue on the 4th string, 4th fret by adding your 3rd finger.

4 Continue as in the diagram, adding your 4th then 2nd fingers.

FIG.104 - B MINOR BARRE - HAND POSITION

Why Barre Chords Are Worth the Effort

Barre chords can be challenging at first, but they unlock the fretboard and offer great sounding chord options.

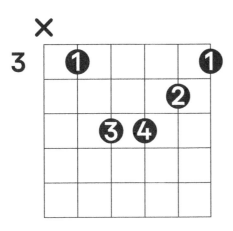

FIG.105 - C MINOR BARRE

Move It Up: C Minor Barre

1 Start on the 5th string at the 3rd fret and position the tip of your 1st finger near the fret.

2 Keeping that fingertip in place, roll your 1st finger across the adjacent strings so you're fretting the 1st string as well.

3 Continue on the 4th string, 5th fret by adding your 3rd finger.

4 Continue as in the diagram, adding your 4th then 2nd fingers.

FIG.106 - C MINOR BARRE - HAND POSITION

BARRE CHORD EXCELLENCE

Do you see a similarity between these two chords?

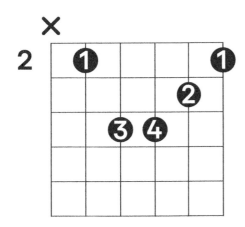

FIG.107 - B MINOR BARRE

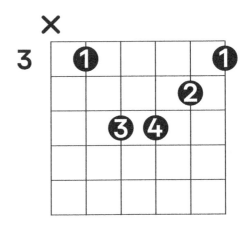

FIG.108 - C MINOR BARRE

You could say they look alike, but begin on different frets. Same shape. Different fretboard locations.

Move It Up Again: D Minor Barre

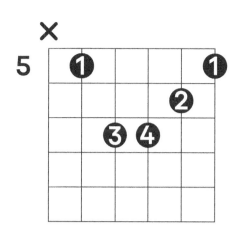

1 Start on the 5th string at the 5th fret and position the tip of your 1st finger near the fret.

2 Keeping that fingertip in place, roll your 1st finger across the adjacent strings so you're fretting the 1st string as well.

FIG.109 - D MINOR BARRE

3 Continue on the 4th string, 7th fret by adding your 3rd finger.

4 Continue as in the diagram, adding your 4th then 2nd fingers.

FIG.110 - D MINOR BARRE - HAND POSITION

6TH STRING MINOR BARRE CHORDS

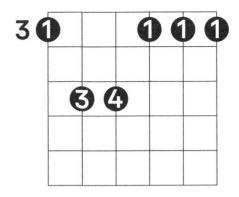

AS YOU COULD PROBABLY GUESS, 6TH-STRING BARRE CHORDS HAVE THEIR LOWEST NOTE ON THE 6TH-STRING.

Remember that barre chords can be moved up and down the neck to instantly create new chords. There are two basic types and you've already learned 5th-String Barre Chords.

FIG.111 - G MINOR BARRE

HOW TO PLAY A 6TH STRING G MINOR BARRE

FIG.112 - G MINOR BARRE - HAND POSITION

1 Start on the 6th string at the 3rd fret. Place your 1st finger there.

2 Now, envision your 1st finger as a log laid across train tracks. Roll this finger downwards, making it lie flat across the adjacent strings.

3 Add your 3rd, then 4th fingers to the 5th fret, as in the diagram.

Barre Chords: A Traveler's Best Friend

Once mastered, barre chords allow you to play in any key, making them invaluable for accompanying singers or playing in different musical keys.

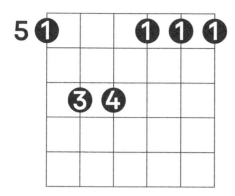

FIG.113 - A MINOR BARRE

FIG.114 - A MINOR BARRE - HAND POSITION

GOING UP:
6TH STRING
B MINOR BARRE

1 Move the A Minor Barre chord up the neck two frets. The lowest note, played by your 1st finger should be on the 6th string at the 7th fret.

Remember that "up the neck" means moving your fretting hand "up" toward the body of the guitar and away from the headstock and nut.

It's considered "up" because the pitches of the neck are higher "up" the neck than "down" by the nut.

UP AND AWAY:
6TH STRING
A MINOR BARRE

You've learned that notes and chords can be played in a variety of locations around the guitar fretboard. Here's yet another way to play A Minor using a 6th-String Barre Chord.

1 This time, start on the 6th string at the 5th fret. Place your 1st finger there.

2 Now, envision your 1st finger as a log laid across train tracks. Roll this finger downwards, making it lie flat across the adjacent strings.

3 Add your 3rd, then 4th fingers as in the diagram.

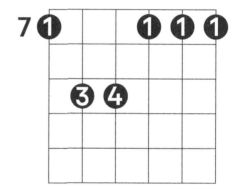

FIG.115 - B MINOR BARRE

FIG.116 - B MINOR BARRE - HAND POSITION

MANY MINOR BARRE CHORDS

6th-String Minor Barre Chords

E min

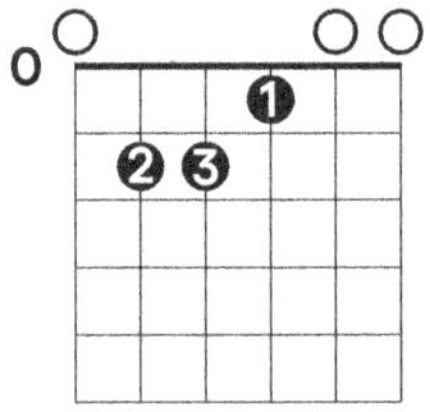

FIG.118 - OPEN-TYPE
E MINOR CHORD

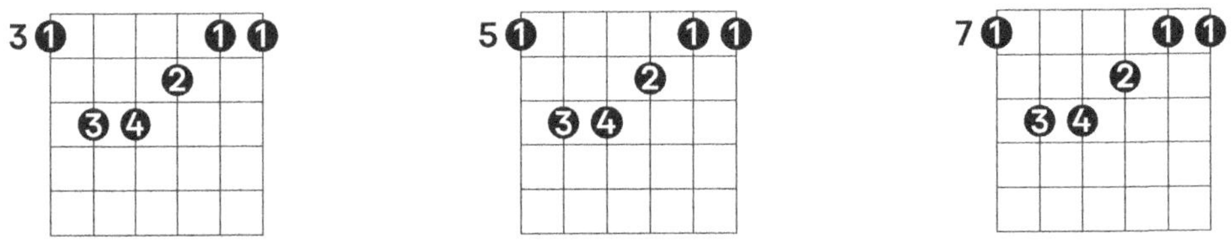

G min   **A min**   **B min**

FIG.119 - 6TH-STRING MINOR BARRE CHORDS

Barre chords can be considered "movable" because the same chord shape "moves" up and down the neck.

Examine these barre chord diagrams and notice that the only detail that changes is the Origin Fret mumber in the upper-corner.

5th-String Minor Barre Chords

A min

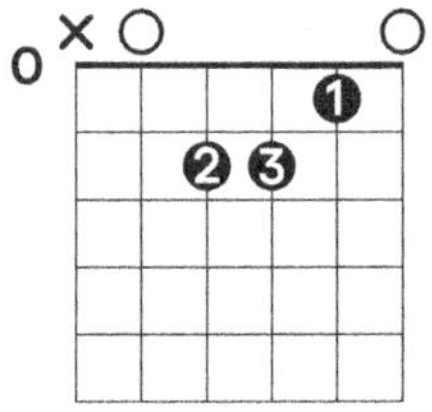

FIG.120 - OPEN-TYPE
A MINOR CHORD

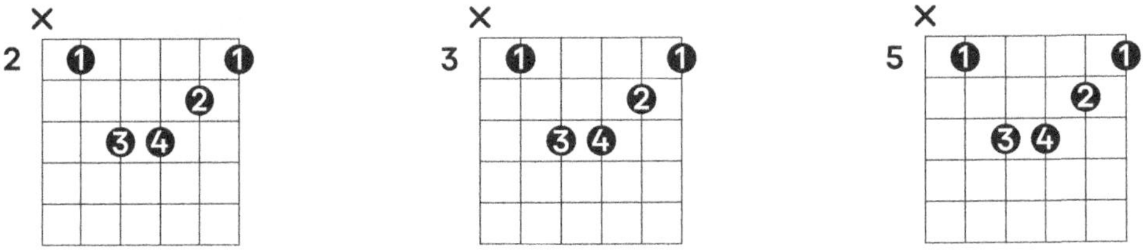

B min   **C min**   **D min**

FIG.121 - 5TH-STRING MINOR BARRE CHORDS

Sonic Flavor: G⁷ and A⁷

G7 AND A7 ARE TWO COLORFUL CHORDS THAT ADD A NEW DIMENSION TO YOUR PLAYING. HAVE A LISTEN TO THEIR RICH AND NUANCED SOUND.

HOW TO PLAY G⁷

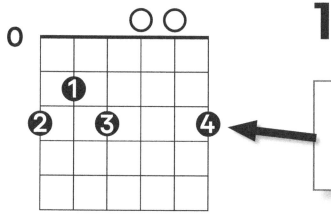

FIG.122 - G7 - FULL

1 Begin by placing your 2nd finger on the 6th string, 3rd fret. The name of this note is G. It's the root of the G Major chord.

> Does this chord shape remind you of G Major? G7 and G Major are nearly alike, but sound SO different!

2 Keeping your finger there, add your 1st finger on the 5th string, 2nd fret.

3 Now, add your 3rd finger to the 4th string, 3rd fret. (Do your fingers feel like a pretzel?)

4 Play the next two strings open.

5 Keeping your other fingers where they are, add your 4th finger on the 1st string, 3rd fret.

6 Strum gently across all the strings, listening for clarity. Adjust your fingers if any note sounds muffled.

FIG.123 - G7 - FULL HAND POSITION

All your fingers were used for that one. How do things sound? Smooth and controlled, or wild and clumsy? Each time you practice, modify your approach until you get controlled notes and tone.

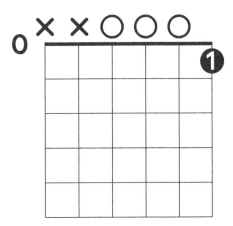

G⁷ - EASY VERSION

FIG.124 - G7 - EASY

Feel like learning a super-great, super-easy one-finger chord? Check out this colorful little nugget.

1 On the 1st string at the 1st fret, place your 1st finger.

2 Strum the 4th through 1st strings. Isn't that pretty?

FIG.125 - G7 - EASY HAND POSITION

Sonic Flavor - The Dominant 7th:

The G7 and A7 chords add a bluesy or jazzy feel to music, often leading back to the tonic chord in a progression. Tonic means "root" and the tonic chord is the key of the song.

Music Theory 101: Any chord name (like A, B, C, etc.) followed by a "7" is called a Dominant 7th.

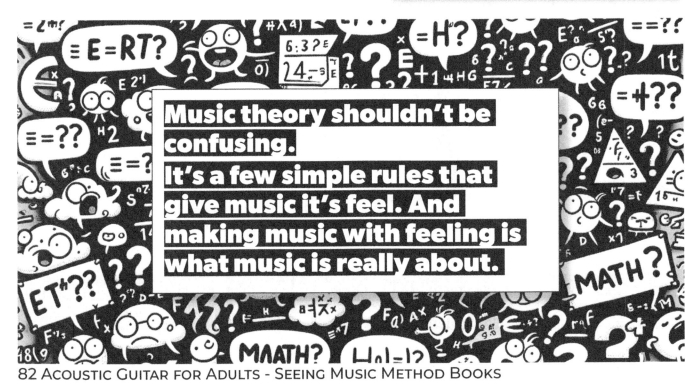

Music theory shouldn't be confusing. It's a few simple rules that give music it's feel. And making music with feeling is what music is really about.

BONUS - MORE G⁷ FINGERINGS

REMEMBER THERE ARE MANY WAYS TO PLAY THE SAME CHORD. INCLUDING THE FULL VERSION YOU'VE ALREADY SEEN, HERE ARE A COUPLE OTHERS.

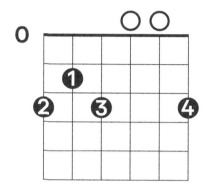

FIG.126 - G7 - TYPE 1

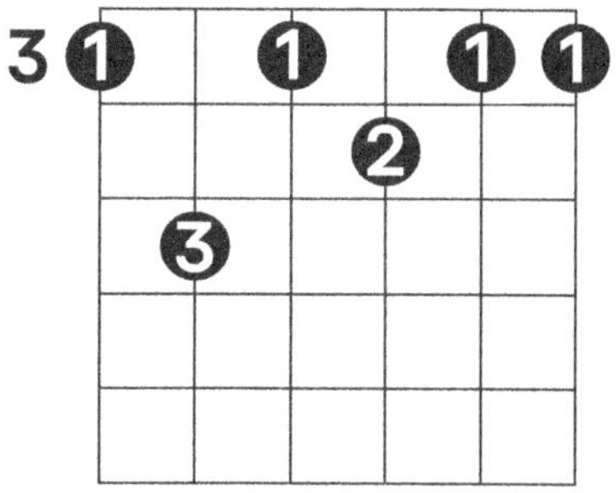

FIG.127 - G7 BARRE

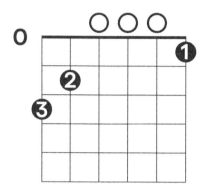

FIG.128 - G7 - TYPE 2

HOW TO PLAY A⁷

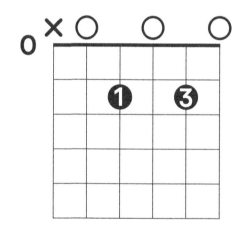

FIG.129 - A7 - FULL

1 Play the root note A with an open 5th string. No fretting finger needed.

2 On the 5th string at the 2nd fret, add your first finger.

3 Let the 3rd string ring open - no fingers needed here!

4 Add the 2nd string, 1st fret with your 3rd finger.

5 Play the 1st string open.

FIG.130 - A7 - FULL HAND POSITION

A⁷ - EASY VERSION

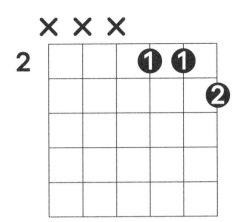

FIG.131 - A7 - EASY

1 On the 3rd string at the 2nd fret, place your 1st finger.

2 Keeping your fingertip there, roll your 1st finger down a bit so you're fretting both the 3rd and 2nd strings.

FIG.132 - A7- EASY HAND POSITION

3 Add your 2nd finger to the 1st string at the 3rd fret. That's it!

Music History: The 1950s

Popular music and Jazz sounded somewhat similar in the '50s. Big bands ruled the dancefloors and radio, with their rich harmonies provided by horn sections, guitar and piano. Both popular music and Jazz rely on G7 and A7, called "seventh chords".

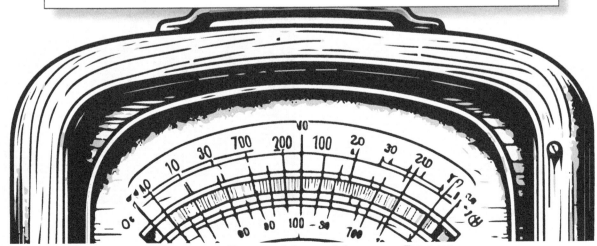

EXERCISES FOR G⁷ AND A⁷

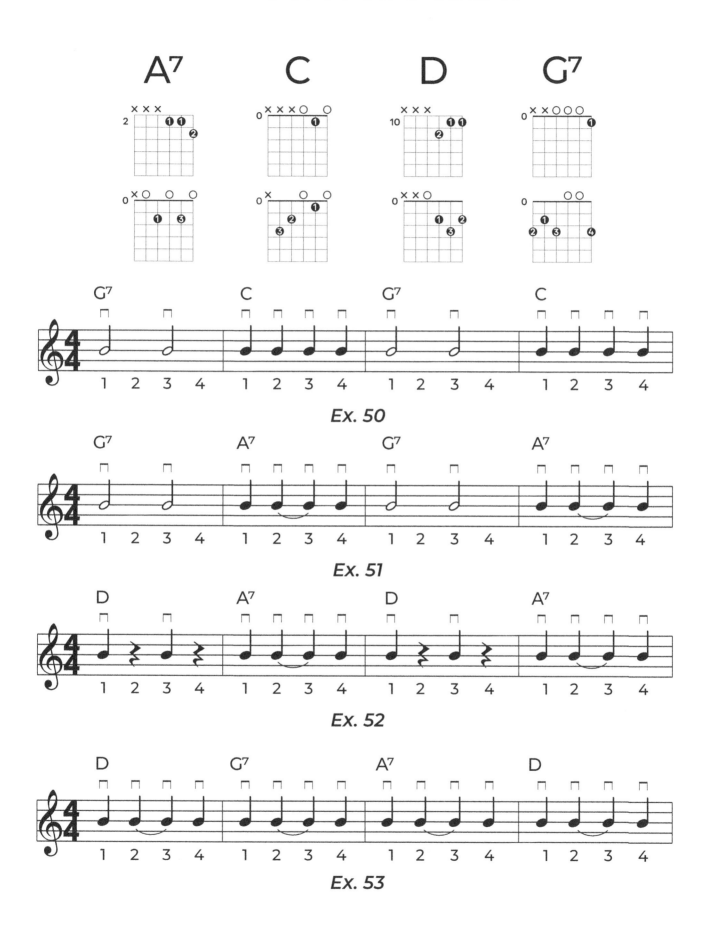

Ex. 50

Ex. 51

Ex. 52

Ex. 53

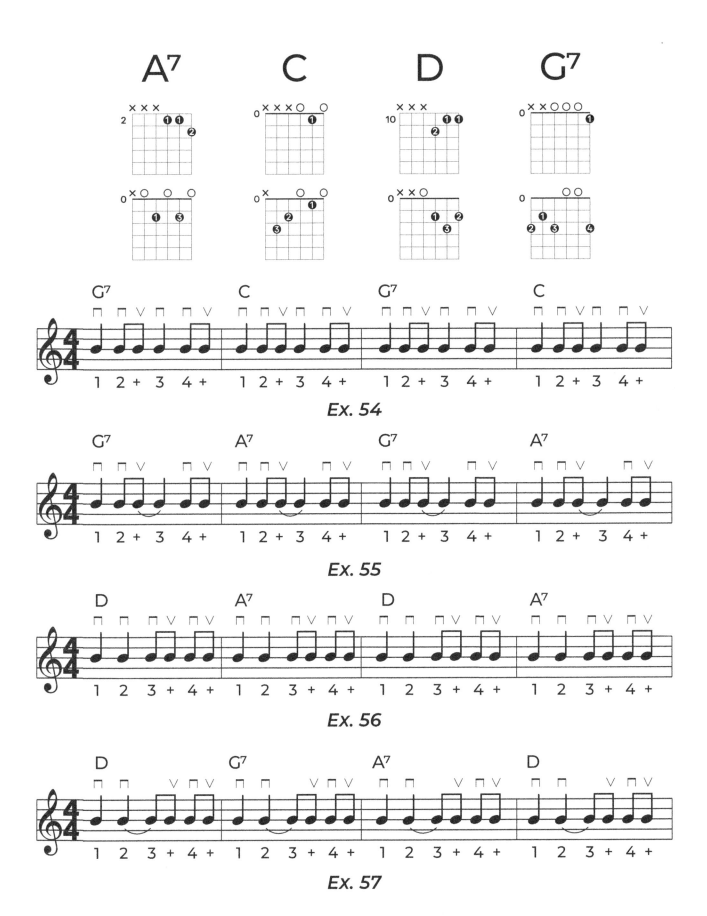

Ex. 54

Ex. 55

Ex. 56

Ex. 57

Classic Cool: C^Maj7 and D^7

LEARN TWO ULTRA-CLASSIC (AND CLASSY!) CHORDS TO IGNITE YOUR MUSIC QUICKLY.

HOW TO PLAY C^MAJ7

C^Maj7 (pron: C Major 7) is a cool, sophisticated chord with beautiful overtones. Listen to them intertwine as you learn this chord.

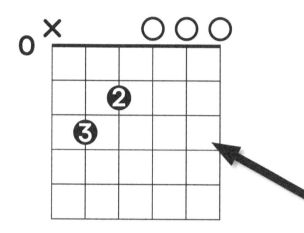

Fig.133 - C Maj7 - Full

1 Begin on the 5th string at the 3rd fret with your 3rd finger. You'll remember this is the root C.

Compare this chord shape to the full C Major chord from earlier. See how they're almost identical?

Identifying similar shapes helps you retain them in your memory.

2 Add the 4th string, 2nd fret, 2nd finger.

3 The next few strings (3rd, 2nd and 1st strings) are played open. This means they should ring freely, so be careful not to inadvertently mute them with your fretting hand.

Fig.134 - C Maj7 - Full Hand Position

Notice how the C Major 7 shape closely resembles a standard C Major chord?

C Major

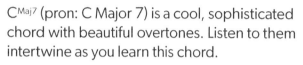

SEEING MUSIC

C^MAJ7 - EASY VERSION

FIG.135 - C MAJOR7 - EASY

1 On the 3rd string at the 5th fret, place your 1st finger. Roll it across both the 3rd and 2nd strings.

2 Add your 3rd finger to the 1st string at the the 7th fret (2 frets higher). Strum from the 3rd string through the 1st.

FIG.136 - C MAJOR7 - EASY HAND POSITION

The Craft of Luthiery

Luthiers are the skilled craftspeople who build and repair stringed instruments, and their work is as much about art as it is about science.

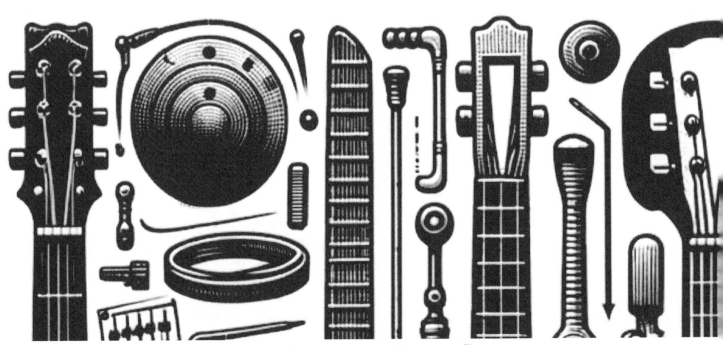

HOW TO PLAY D⁷

1 Play the 4th string open. This is open D.

2 On the 3rd string at the 2nd fret, add your 2nd finger.

3 On the 2nd string at the 1st fret, add your 1st finger.

4 Finally, add your 3rd finger. This is on the 1st string at the 2nd fret.

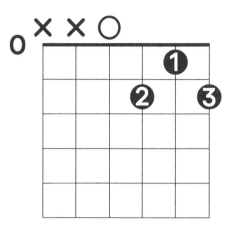

Fig.137 - D7 - Full

Fig.138 - D7 - Full Hand Position

Q&A: Why are some chords written with just a "7" and others a "Maj7"?

The extension, 7 or Maj7, indicate two different sets of notes, which will require different fingerings and also have a different sounds.

D⁷ - EASY VERSION

1 On the 3rd string at the 7th fret, place your 1st finger and roll it down across the 2nd string, as well.

2 Add your 2nd finger. It goes on the 1st string at the 8th fret (one fret higher).

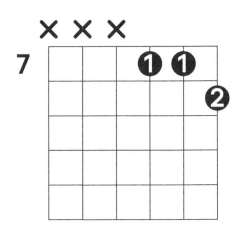

FIG.139 - D7 - EASY

FIG.140 - D7- EASY HAND POSITION

Why Two Different 7's?

Major 7th and Dominant 7th chords bring distinct colors to music.

The first is more laid-back, while the Dominant-type drives tension and release.

UNDERSTANDING 3/4 TIME

While you might be familiar with the 4/4 time signature where each measure consists of four quarter-notes, another commonly used time signature is **3/4**. Pronounced *"three-four"* or *"three-quarter time"*, 3/4 time incorporates three quarter-notes in each measure. This signature is quintessential for waltzes, lending them their distinctive rhythmic pattern.

FIG.141 - TREBLE CLEF AND 3/4 TIME SIGNATURE

Exercises in 3/4 Time

Now put your knowledge into action by playing a basic waltz using just the C Major chord. Remember the finger placements discussed previously for each chord.

1 Strum each chord three times per measure, maintaining a consistent downstroke pattern.

2 Aim to transition smoothly between the chords. Keep a steady, controlled rhythm.

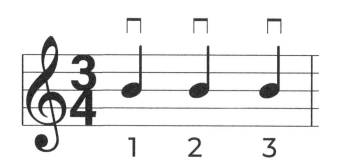

FIG.142 - ONE MEASURE OF 3/4

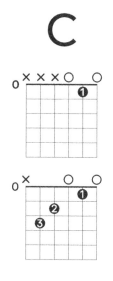

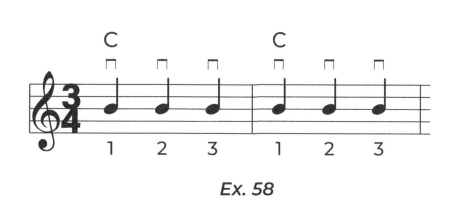

Ex. 58

More Than "Just a Waltz"

Here's a collection of mini-songs using 3/4 time. While you may hear yourself playing a Waltz, it's just as likely these exercises will remind you of Country or Pop or even Jazz. Try playing them very softly, then strongly at a medium-loud volume.

The volume of music in a song is called **dynamics** and it's essential to making great music.

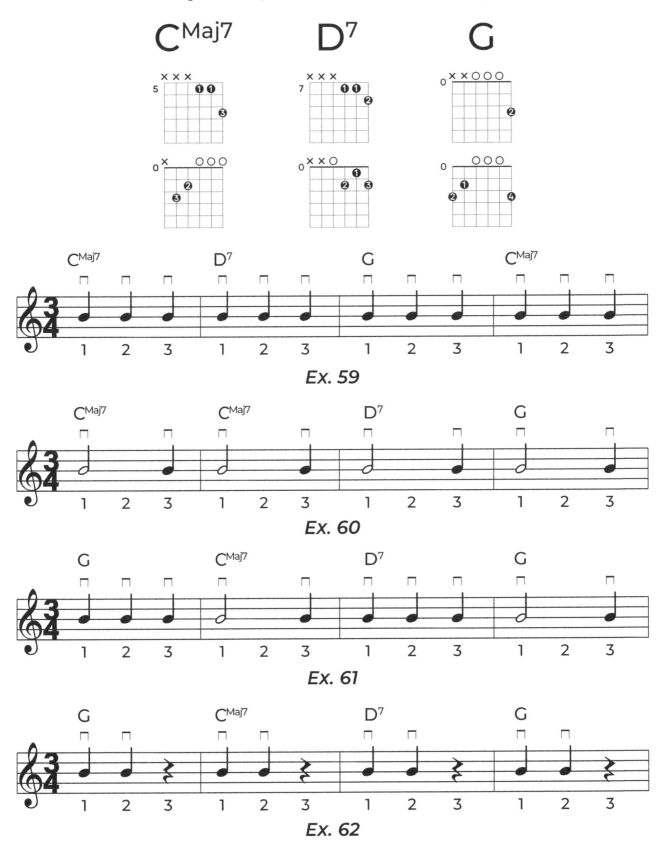

Ex. 59

Ex. 60

Ex. 61

Ex. 62

It's About Tone

Why Your Guitar's Wood Matters: Tone, Resonance, and Response

Whether you're strumming or picking an acoustic guitar, you're not just using a hand tool — you're interacting with a piece of craftsmanship where every detail matters — especially the wood. Here's why:

Tonal Qualities

Top Wood (Soundboard): The wood used for the top of the guitar, also known as the soundboard, is crucial for tone. Spruce is commonly used because of its strength-to-weight ratio, which offers a balanced tone that's bright and responsive. Cedar, on the other hand, is softer with a warmer sound, often favored in fingerstyle playing.

Back and Sides: Rosewood is popular for the back and sides of a guitar, imparting a rich, resonant bass and complex harmonics. Mahogany, with a more straightforward, punchy sound, emphasizes the midrange and is often used in blues and folk music.

Resonance and Projection

Each wood type has a unique density and stiffness that contribute to the guitar's resonance. Maple, for instance, has lower internal damping, leading to a clearer, more focused sound with less overtones.

The guitar body's size and shape also interact with the wood's resonance characteristics, affecting the instrument's projection and volume. Bigger bodies generally sound bigger.

Sustain and Dynamic Response

The wood's hardness affects sustain — the duration your note rings out. Hardwoods like ebony and rosewood, used for fretboards, can enhance sustain.

When used in body construction, softwoods like spruce can offer a quick response to a light touch, while hardwoods may require a more forceful strike to reveal their full tonal spectrum.

Aesthetics and Durability

Woods like rosewood and maple not only sound different but also offer unique grains and colors, contributing to the visual appeal of the instrument.

Durability is another factor. Hardwoods like rosewood and mahogany can withstand the rigors of climate changes and playing, affecting the longevity of the guitar.

EVERY MUSICIAN HAS A FAVORITE STYLE OR GENRE. FIND YOURS HERE AND DIG IN TO A STRUMMING PATTERN YOU'LL ENJOY.

OLD-TIME CLASSICS

This quarter rest is a "Pick-Up Note". It's the lead-in beat of the song.

The vocal sings it alone, then you strum beginning at the next measure.

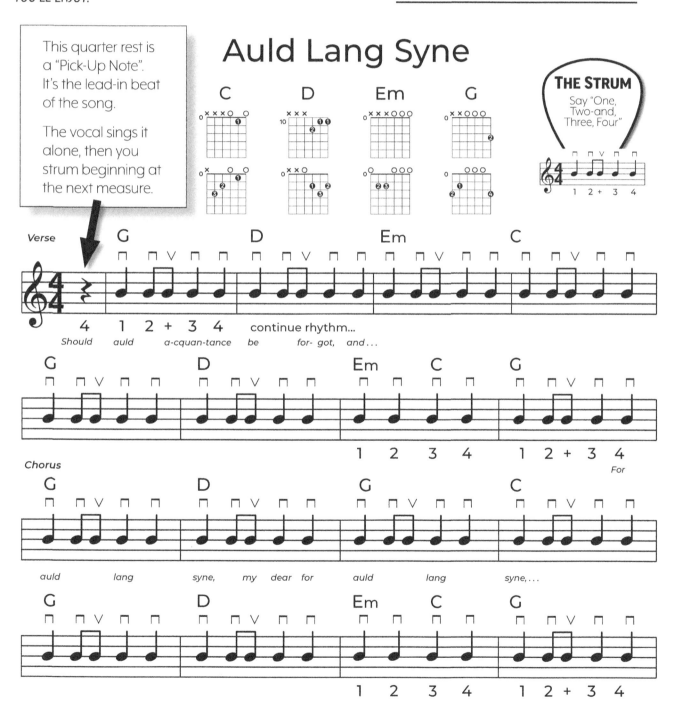

Auld Lang Syne

THE STRUM
Say "One, Two-and, Three, Four"

Verse

Should auld a-cquan-tance be for- got, and . . .

continue rhythm...

auld lang syne, my dear for auld lang syne, . . .

Chorus

For

The Star Spangled Banner

America - God Save the King

Heads-Up!: Only two measures on this line.

Music History

"The Star-Spangled Banner" was officially adopted as the national anthem of the United States on March 3, 1931, by a congressional resolution which was signed into law by President Herbert Hoover. The song's lyrics were written by Francis Scott Key in 1814 during the War of 1812, and it was set to the tune of a popular British song of the time called "To Anacreon in Heaven."

Swing Low, Sweet Chariot

Traditional Spiritual

Swing Low, sweet cha- ri- ot

continue rhythm...

looked over Jor- dan and what did I see?....

Lyrics: I

Notice that several measures contain two chords. Practice very slowly until shifting your fingers becomes easy.

Rock, Roll and Rumble

See how the rhythm changes in the 1st, 5th and 16th measures? In those measures, stop your strings on beat 4.

THE STRUM
Say "One, Two-and, Three, Four-and"

Guitar in the '50s:

The '50s saw the rise of the guitar as an icon of rock 'n' roll with pioneers like Chuck Berry.

Soda Shop Twist

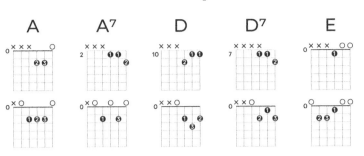

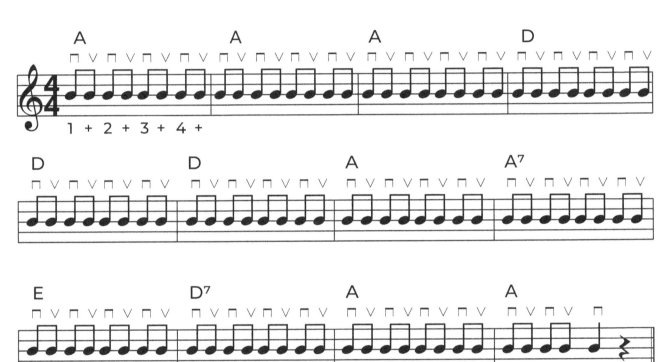

> Rhythm was all-important to 1950s jukebox hits. Hit songs had a unique and memorable beat, often made for dancing

Jukebox Diner Jam

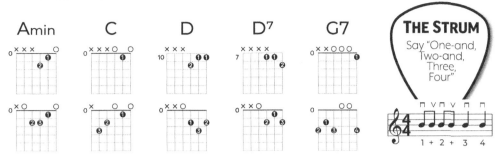

60'S POP

California Summer Cruise

Light Swing

Surf Tunes

Mrs. Robinson Loves You

The 1960s were a melting pot of sound and songs. While folk singers strummed the chords of change, the rock and pop scenes exploded with a kaleidoscope of sounds. The Beatles and The Rolling Stones brought the British Invasion to the shores of the U.S., while Motown artists like The Supremes and The Temptations gave voice to a new era of soul. The '60s was truly a decade where music was as diverse as the rapidly changing world.

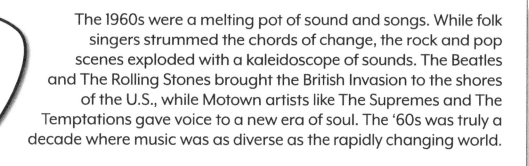

Sit In, Unplug, Play On

The Folk Revival of the 1960s

The 1960s folk revival brought acoustic guitar to the forefront as a symbol of counterculture and social commentary.

Saturday Nights Alive

The '70s and the Singer-Songwriter Era

The '70s brought the rise of the singer-songwriter, where the acoustic guitar played a key role in the introspective storytelling of artists like James Taylor.

Jeanie Blue Eyes

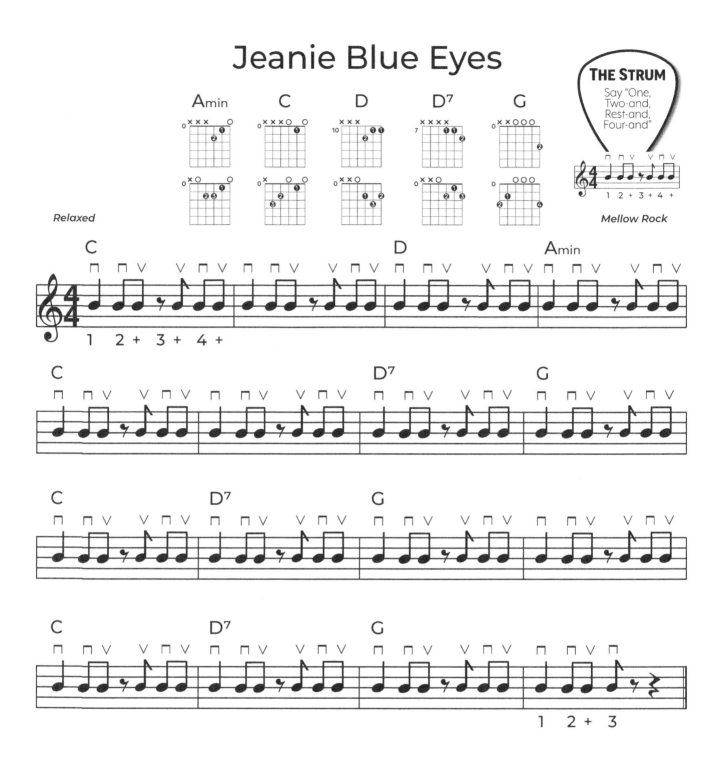

Bird of Freedom

Rock Against War

The Vietnam War left a deep imprint on the Rock music of the 1970s. Lyrics became more politically charged, reflecting the unrest and the desire for peace. Bands like Creedence Clearwater Revival and singers like John Lennon became voices of a generation, using their music as a form of protest and to galvanize anti-war sentiment. The era's Rock not only entertained but also empowered and united people during one of the most tumultuous periods in modern history.

80'S RADIO

Valley Life Dolls

Bouncy, Upbeat

Totally Tubular

The Eighties: The Era of Big Hair and Bold Chords

The '80s might be known for electric guitar solos, but acoustic guitar ballads and chord progressions were also central to the decade's sound.

Galactic Groove

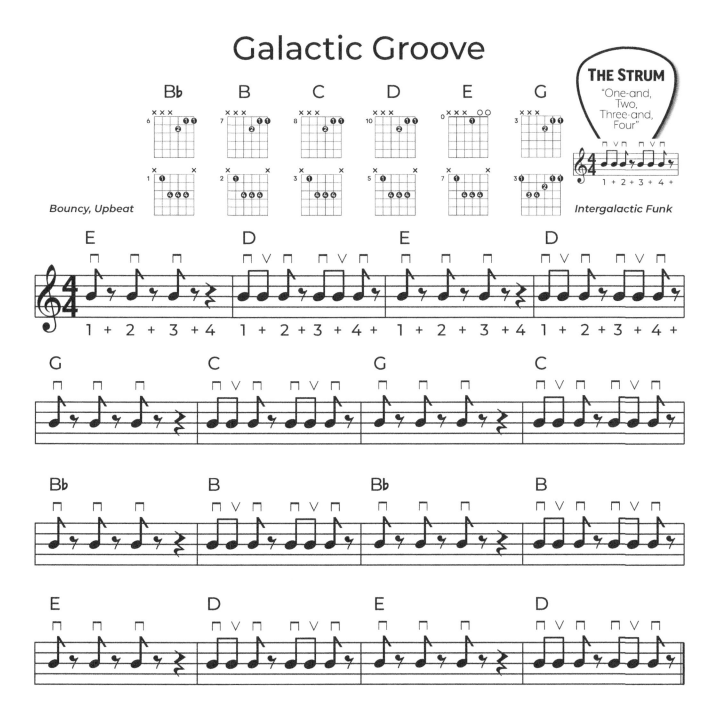

Funk's Acoustic Echo

"Funk's infectious grooves and syncopated rhythms didn't just electrify dance floors in its heyday—it also left a lasting legacy on the acoustic world. Modern troubadours like Ed Sheeran draw from funk's rhythmic complexity to create percussive, groove-laden acoustic hits. By tapping, slapping, and employing fingerstyle techniques, they turn the acoustic guitar into a one-person band, showcasing how funk's spirit continues to inspire across genres and generations."

Lunar Dreamer

Midnight Mirage

This Van Needs an Air Freshener

The '90s: Unplugged Sessions

MTV's Unplugged series highlighted the acoustic guitar's integral role in rock and pop music. Soon, acoustic music found a broad audience in coffee shops, campuses and music festivals.

Disco, Ball

Walk of Shame

(She's a) Pop Princess

OLD-TIME COUNTRY & AMERICANA

Amazing Grace

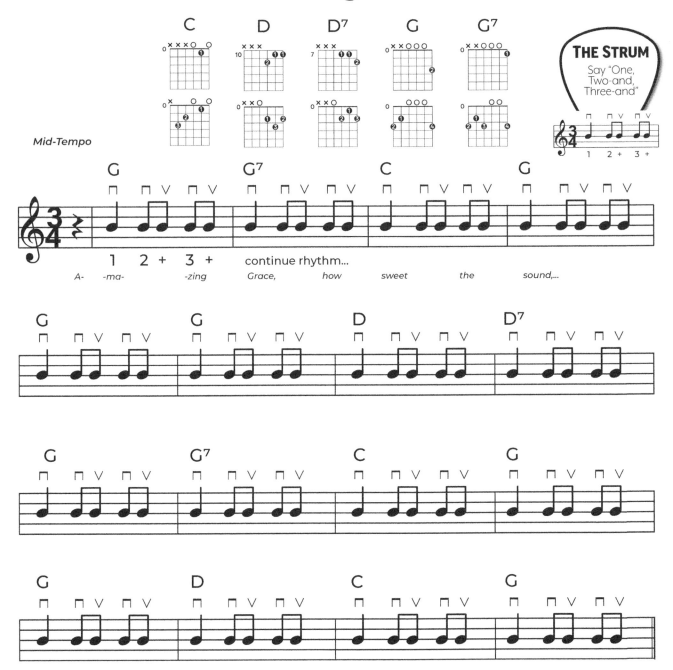

Music History

"Amazing Grace" is one of the most recorded songs in history, with over 11,000 versions documented. Its timeless message and melody have resonated with artists from Aretha Franklin to Elvis Presley.

Whiskey, Wagons, Wheels

Outlaw Country: The Renegades of Nashville

"Outlaw Country emerged in the 1970s as a rebellion against the polished Nashville sound. Led by mavericks like Willie Nelson and Waylon Jennings, these artists broke from mainstream country's constraints, producing music that was raw, honest, and reflected their rugged lifestyles. The term 'Outlaw' was coined from their nonconformity to the industry norms and their songs that often celebrated the outlaw persona.

A Cowboy on One Knee

Country Music and the Acoustic Guitar

Country music and acoustic guitars have a deep connection, with the instrument's twangy and heartfelt sound defining the genre.

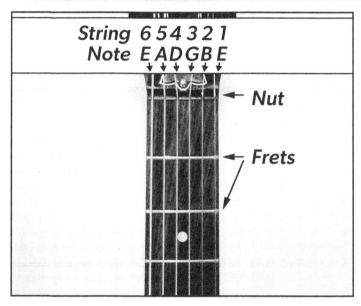

FIG.143 - STANDARD GUITAR TUNING

Common Guitar Tunings

Standard	E A D G B E
Std. Lowered	Eb Ab Db Gb Bb Eb
DADGAD	D A D G A D
Drop D	D A D G B E
Open G	D G D G B D

FIG.144 - COMMON GUITAR TUNINGS

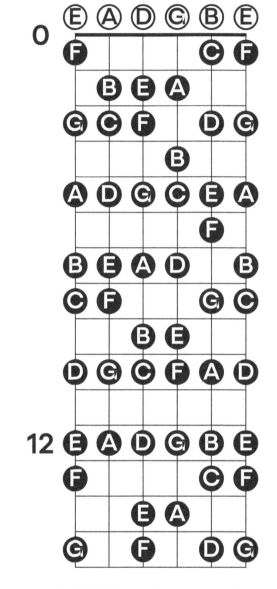

FIG.146 - NATURAL NOTES OF THE GUITAR

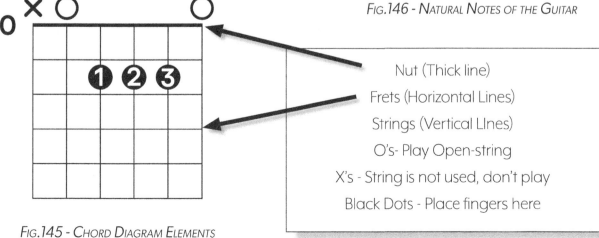

Nut (Thick line)

Frets (Horizontal Lines)

Strings (Vertical LInes)

O's- Play Open-string

X's - String is not used, don't play

Black Dots - Place fingers here

FIG.145 - CHORD DIAGRAM ELEMENTS

A Major

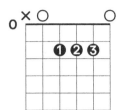 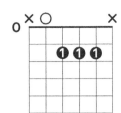 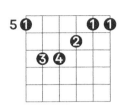 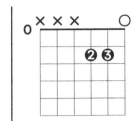 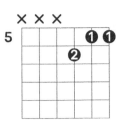

A Minor

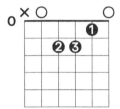 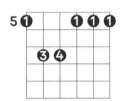 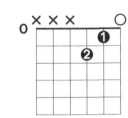

A7

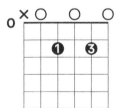  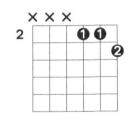

B-flat Major

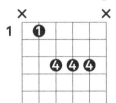 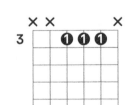 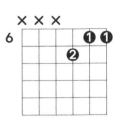

B Major

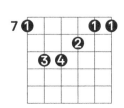 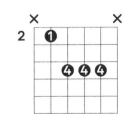 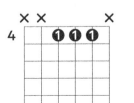 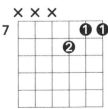

B Minor

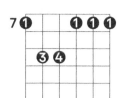 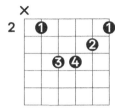 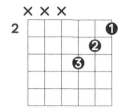

C Major

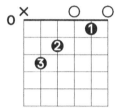 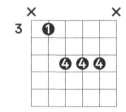 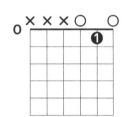 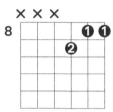

C Minor

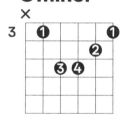

C⁷

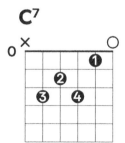 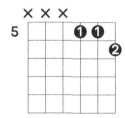

C^{Maj7}

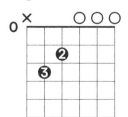 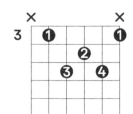 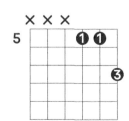

Open-String or Barre

Easy

D Major

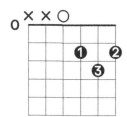 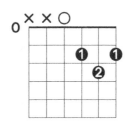 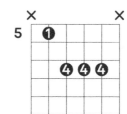

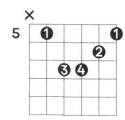

D Minor

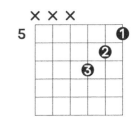

D7

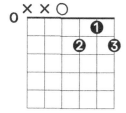 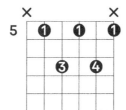

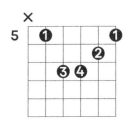

E Major

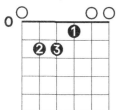

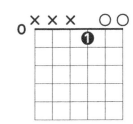

E Minor

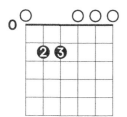

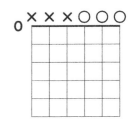

F Major

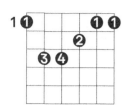

G Major

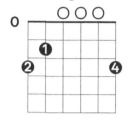 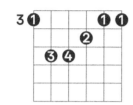 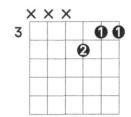 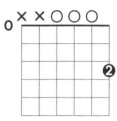

G Minor

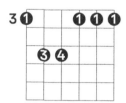 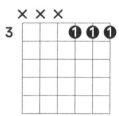

G7

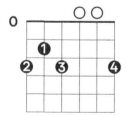 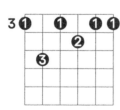 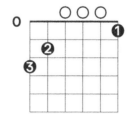 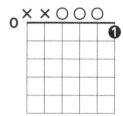

Thanks and congratulations on your purchase of this book! Here are your streaming lesson videos.

Visit: https://seeingmusicbooks.com/x86rt2m2m

1 For access to the lesson videos, scan this QR or visit the URL above

2 Register for our website, FREE at seeingmusicbooks.com

3 Watch the lesson videos on any computer or device logged-in to seeingmusicbooks.com

Made in the USA
Las Vegas, NV
28 March 2024

87876411R10070